Artificial Intelligence on the Sinclair QL

Make your micro think

Keith and Steven Brain

First published 1984 by:
Sunshine Books (an imprint of Scot Press Ltd.)
12–13 Little Newport Street
London WC2R 3LD

British Library Cataloguing in Publication Data

Brain, K.R.
    Artificial intelligence on the Sinclair QL.
    1. Artificial intelligence—Data processing
    2. Sinclair QL (Computer)
    I. Title   II. Brain, Steven
    001.53'5'0285404   Q336

    ISBN 0-946408-41-6

Cover design by Grad Graphic Design Ltd.
Cover illustration by Stuart Hughes.
Typeset by Paragon Photoset, Aylesbury.
Printed in Great Britain by Short Run Press Ltd, Exeter.

CONTENTS

Contents in detail

CHAPTER 7
Fuzzy Matching
Recovering information from the human mind — soundex coding — a program for converting names — retrieving information.

CHAPTER 8
Recognising Shapes
Simulating the action of a light sensor — looking at a smaller number of features of the pattern.

CHAPTER 9
An Intelligent Teacher
Questions and answers — keeping a score — shifting the emphasis of questions to areas of difficulty — making questions easier or harder.

CHAPTER 10
Of Mice and Men
Setting the scene — making the maze — finding the route — reaching the centre — deciding where to move to — coping with corners — reducing the amount of checking — random selection at junctions — backtracking — finding new routes — speeding up.

CHAPTER 11
Intelligent Use of Archive
Extracting the required information correctly — finding a match — searching specifically — selecting records — putting things in order — using PROCedures — a more friendly (inter)face.

CHAPTER 12
A Naturally Expert Salesman
Combining processing natural language with an expert system — making conversation with the computer — making decisions — the Computer Salesman.

Program Notes

The order of the X and Y coordinates in the 'AT' command vary with the version of the ROM. If the screen organisation looks wrong, then simply reverse the two parameters following AT.

Introduction

Artificial intelligence is undoubtedly an increasingly important area in computer development and one which will have profound effects on all our lives in the next few decades. The main aim of this book is to introduce the unenlightened reader to some of the concepts involved in artificial intelligence and to show them how to develop 'intelligent' routines on the QL which they can then incorporate into their own particular programs. Only a superficial knowledge of programming is assumed and the book works from first principles as we believe that this is essential if you are really to understand the problems involved in simulating intelligence, and how to set about overcoming them.

The basic format of the book is that ideas are taken and suitable routines built up step by step, exploring and comparing alternative possibilities wherever possible. Rather than simply giving you a series of completed programs, we encourage you to experiment with different approaches to let you see the results of variations in technique for yourself. Detailed flowcharts of most of the routines are included.

Although the main emphasis is placed on the AI aspects of the routines, we have taken the opportunity to exploit many of the advantages of SuperBASIC, such as PROCedures, FuNctions, and Windows.

You may notice that in places certain lines are strictly redundant, but these have been deliberately included in the interests of clarity of program flow. As far as possible, retyping of lines is strenuously avoided but modification of routines is commonplace. Certain defined PROCedures are common to several chapters and we remind you that these can be SAVEd separately to microdrive and then transferred into the different programs with the MERGE command.

All listings in the book are formatted so that they clearly show nesting and program flow, and so they do not appear exactly as they will on the screen display. In most cases spaces and brackets have been used liberally to make listings easier to read but be warned that some spaces and brackets are essential so do not be tempted to remove them all.

All routines have been rigorously tested and the listings have been checked very thoroughly so we hope that you will not find any bugs. It is a sad fact of life that most bugs arise as a result of 'tryping mitsakes' by the user. Semicolons and commas may look insignificant but their absence can have profound effects!

Artificial intelligence is increasing in importance every day and we hope that this book will give you a useful insight into the area. Who knows — if you really work at the subject you might be able to persuade your machine to read our next book for itself!

Once again thanks are due to Liz who has managed to resist the temptation to throw out 'all that rubbish' and redecorate the room.

Keith and Steven Brain
Groeswen, July 1984

CHAPTER 1
Artificial Intelligence

Fantasy

For generations science fiction writers have envisaged the development of intelligent machines which could carry out many of the functions of man himself (or even surpass him in some areas), and the public image of artificial intelligence has undoubtedly been coloured by these images.

The most common view of a robot is that it is an intelligent machine of generally anthropomorphic (human) form which is capable of independently carrying out instructions which are given to it in only a very general manner. Of course, most people have ingrained Luddite tendencies when it comes to technology so in the early stories these robots tended to have a very bad press, being cast in the traditional role of the 'bad guys' but with near-invincibility and lack of conscience built in.

The far-sighted Isaac Asimov wove a lengthy series of stories around his concept of 'positronic robots' and was probably the first author really to get to grips with the realities of the situation. He laid down his famous 'Three Laws of Robotics' which specified the basic ground rules which must be built into any machine which is capable of independent action — but it is interesting to note that he could not see the time when the human race would accept the presence of such robots on the earth itself. 'Star Wars' introduced the specialised robots R2D2 and C3PO, but we feel that many of their design features were a little strange: perhaps there is a 'Interplanetary Union of Robots' and a demarcation dispute prevented direct communication between humans and R2D2.

Of course intelligent computers also appear in boxes without arms and legs, although flashing lights seem obligatory. Input/output must obviously be vocal but the old metallic voice has clearly gone out of fashion in favour of some more definite personality. If all the boxes look the same then this must be a good idea, but please don't make them all sound like Sergeant-Major Zero from 'Terrahawks'!

Michael Knight's KITT sounds like a reasonable sort of machine to converse with, and it is certainly preferable to the oily SLAVE and obnoxious ORAC from 'Blake's Seven'. ORAC seemed to pack an enormous amount of scorn into that little perspex box but other writers have appreciated the difficulties which may be produced if you make the personality of the machine too close to that of man himself. In Arthur C.

3

Clarke's '2001: A Space Odyssey' the ultimately-intelligent computer HAL eventually had a nervous breakdown when he faced too many responsibilities. In 'The Restaurant At The End of The Universe' the value of the 'Sirius Cybernetics Corporation Happy Vertical People Transporter' was reduced significantly when it refused to go up as it could see into the future and realised that if it did so it was likely to get zapped, and the 'Nutri-Matic Drinks Synthesiser' was obviously designed by British Rail Catering as it always produced a drink that was 'almost, but not quite, entirely unlike tea'. More recently the rather flashy holographic figure of 'Automan' has demonstrated some quite amazing capabilities in his fight against crime, although there do seem to be some major omissions in his programming with regard to dealings with women.

More worrying themes have also recently appeared. The most significant feature of 'Wargames' was not that someone tapped into JOSHUA (the US Defence Computer) but that once the machine started playing thermonuclear war it wouldn't stop until someone had won the game. In 'The Forbin Project' the US and Russian computers got together and decided that humans are pretty irrelevant anyway.

Reality

The definition and recognition of machine intelligence is the subject of fast and furious debate amongst the experts in the subject. The most generally accepted definition is that first proposed by Alan Turing way back in the late 1940s when computers were the size of houses and even rarer than a slide-rule is today. Rather than trying to lay down a series of criteria which must be satisfied, he took a much broader view of the problem. He reasoned that most human beings accept that most other human beings are intelligent and that therefore if someone cannot determine whether they are dealing with another man or woman, or only a computer, then they must accept that the machine is intelligent. This forms the basis of the famous 'Turing Test' in which an operator has to hold a two-way conversation with another entity via a keyboard and try to get the other party to reveal whether it is actually a machine or just another human being — very awkward!

Many fictional stories circulate about this test, but our favourite is the one where a job applicant is set down in front of a keyboard and left to carry on by himself. Of course he realises the importance of this test to his career prospects and so he struggles valiantly to find the secret, apparently without success. However, after some time the interviewer returns, shakes him by the hand, and congratulates him with the words: 'Well done, old man, the machine couldn't tell if you were human so you are just what we need as one of Her Majesty's Tax Inspectors!'

Everyone has heard from the TV advertisements that the use of computer-aided design techniques is now very common and that in-dustrial robots are almost the sole inhabitants of car production lines (leading to the car window sticker which claims 'Designed by a computer, built by a robot, and driven by an idiot'). In fact most of these industrial robots are really of minimal intelligence as they simply follow a pre-defined pathway without making very much in the way of actual decisions. Even the impressive paint-spraying robot which faithfully follows the pattern it learns when a human operator manually moves its arm cannot learn to deal with a new object without further human intervention.

On the other hand the coming generation of robots have more sophisticated sensors and software which allow them to determine the shape, colour, and texture of objects, and to make more rational decisions. Anyone who has seen reports of the legendary 'Micromouse' contests where definitely non-furry electric vermin scurry independently and purposefully (?) to the centre of a maze will not be amazed by our faith in the future of the intelligent robot, although there seems little point in giving it two arms and two legs.

Another important area where artificial intelligence is being currently exploited is in the field of expert systems, many of which can do as well (or even better) than human experts, especially if you are thinking about weather forecasting. These systems can be experts on any number of things but, in particular, they are of increasing importance in medical diagnosis and treatment — although the medical profession doesn't have to worry too much as there will always be a place for them since 'computers can't cuddle'.

A major barrier to wider use of computers is the ignorance and pigheadedness of the users, who will only as a last resort read the instructions, and expect the machine to be able to understand all their little peculiarities. Processing of 'natural language' is therefore a major growth area and the 'fifth generation' of computers will be much more user-friendly.

Most of the serious work on AI uses more suitable (but exotic) languages, such as LISP and PROLOG, but unfortunately these tend to be pretty unintelligible to the average user! The SuperBASIC routines which follow cannot be expected to give you the key to world domination, although they should give you a reasonable appreciation of the possibilities and problems which artificial intelligence brings. Like all specialists, the experts in AI have their own technical jargon with which to impress the ignorant natives. However, as this book is squarely aimed at the edification of Mr/Ms Average, we have deliberately chosen to avoid the use of such jargon wherever possible, as we feel that it tends to confuse rather than aid the novice!

CHAPTER 2
Just Following Orders

As your computer is actually totally unintelligent, you can really only converse with it at a relatively basic level, and in a formally structured way. We will demonstrate later how you can try to break down this 'language barrier', but let's make sure we can walk before we try to run. The first step is to have a series of preset orders to which there are fixed responses.

We will start by examining the problems involved in making the computer understand you giving it compass directions. At first sight the simplest way to program this appears to be to form a REPeat loop which asks for an INPUT from the user and contains a separate IF–THEN line for each possibility (see **Flowchart 2.1**).

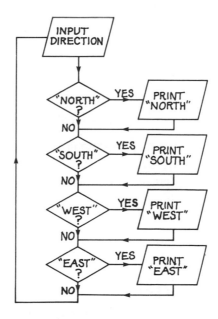

Flowchart 2.1:   Giving Compass Directions.

We will use two PROCedures, which will be steadily refined as the chapter progresses. For the moment, START just clears the screen, whilst WHICHWAY does the work of comparing your input with four key command words.

```
   10 START
   20 WHICHWAY

10000 DEFine PROCedure START
10010    CLS
10990 END DEFine START

11000 DEFine PROCedure WHICHWAY
11010    REPeat DIRECTION
11020       UNDER 0 : PRINT \"DIRECTION?"
11030       INPUT IN$ : UNDER 1
11100       IF IN$="NORTH" THEN PRINT "NORTH"
11110       IF IN$="SOUTH" THEN PRINT "SOUTH"
11120       IF IN$="WEST" THEN PRINT "WEST"
11130       IF IN$="EAST" THEN PRINT "EAST"
11980    END REPeat DIRECTION
11990 END DEFine WHICHWAY
```

To distinguish clearly between your INPUT and the response from the QL we have arranged for the response to be UNDERlined, whilst the backslash before 'DIRECTION' forces a new line.

A problem case?

When you test this routine you will soon find a common problem — the computer only matches upper case (capital) letters, as strings are compared *exactly*.

Thus, while 'NORTH' equals 'NORTH' and 'north' equals 'north', 'north' cannot equal 'NORTH'.

The simplest thing to do is to just check if the first character of IN$ is upper case. All capitals have CODEs less than 91 so a large prompt could be displayed, when necessary, reminding you to press CAPSLOCK.

```
11040       IF CODE(IN$)>90 THEN
11050          CSIZE 2,1 : PRINT "press CAPSLOCK!"
             : CSIZE 1,0
11060          NEXT DIRECTION
11070       END IF
```

(In SuperBASIC there is no need to specify the first letter (IN$(1)) as CODE will return the value for the first character in a string unless a different point is specified.)

A more sophisticated approach is to persuade the computer to automatically convert all letters entered into a particular case. To understand how this operates we need to look at the binary representation of the letters (see **Table 2.1**). You will notice that the only difference between corresponding upper and lower case letters is that bit 6 (= 32) is always set in lower case but reset in upper case.

Table 2.1:   **Binary Representation of Upper and Lower Case Letters.**

bit	8	7	6	5	4	3	2	1
value	128	64	32	16	8	4	2	1
A	0	1	0	0	0	0	0	1
B	0	1	0	0	0	0	1	0
Y	0	1	0	1	1	0	0	1
Z	0	1	0	1	1	0	1	0
a	0	1	1	0	0	0	0	1
b	0	1	1	0	0	0	1	0
y	0	1	1	1	1	0	0	1
z	0	1	1	1	1	0	1	0

To force both upper and lower case characters into lower case, we therefore need to ensure that bit 6 is always set: to perform the opposite conversion, we need to ensure that bit 32 is not set (that it is reset).

To set bit 6, we need to perform a 'bitwise OR' on the character code. This sets bit 6 whether it was already set OR not.

For example:

```
'A' = 65                        01000001
bitwise OR 32                   00100000
                                --------
                                01100001 = 97 ('a')


'a' = 97                        01100001
bitwise OR 32                   00100000
                                --------
                                01100001 = 97 ('a')
```

To reset bit 6 we should perform a 'bitwise NOT' on the character code. This resets bit 6 whether or NOT it was set.

For example:

'A' = 65	01000001
bitwise NOT 32	00100000

$$01000001 = 65 \text{ ('A')}$$

'a' = 97	01100001
bitwise NOT 32	00100000

$$01000001 = 65 \text{ ('A')}$$

We will DEFine a FuNction called GET$ which will perform either conversion. This uses only the bitwise OR command of the QL for two reasons. The first (very practical) reason is that our QL, at least, doesn't recognise the bitwise NOT command even though it is in the manual! The second reason is that it is then possible to use a single function to convert from lower case to upper case or vice versa simply by passing a parameter.

The GET$ function is called from line 11030 which replaces the old INPUT line and prompt.

```
11030 IN$=GET$(1) : UNDER 1
11040 REMark DELETED
11050 REMark DELETED
11060 REMark DELETED
11070 REMark DELETED
```

The parameter passed (cs) must be either 0 or 1 where 0 indicates conversion to lower case, and 1 conversion to upper case.

An INPUT (i$) is made as usual, but then the REPeat GET_CHAR loop takes each character in turn (i$ (n)) and this has a bitwise OR ($\frac{||}{||}$) with 32 performed on it. This forces bit 6 to be set. However the value of 32*cs (the parameter passed) is now subtracted from the result. If cs is zero then this will have no effect and lower case will be produced. But if cs is 1 then 32 will be subtracted, which will effectively reset bit 6, whether it was originally set or NOT, and produce upper case. If the end of the INPUT is reached (n=LEN (i$)) we EXIT GET_CHAR and the result (r$) is RETurned to the calling line as IN$ (see **Flowchart 2.2**).

```
20000 DEFine FuNction GET$(cs)
20010    LOCal i$,n,t$,r$
```

```
20020     n=1
20030     r$=" "
20040     INPUT i$
20050       REPeat GET_CHAR
20060         t$=i$(n)
20070         r$=r$ & CHR$((CODE(t$) || 32)-
              (32*cs))
20080           IF n=LEN(i$) THEN EXIT GET_CHAR
20090         n=n+1
20100       END REPeat GET_CHAR
20110     RETurn r$
20120 END DEFine GET$
```

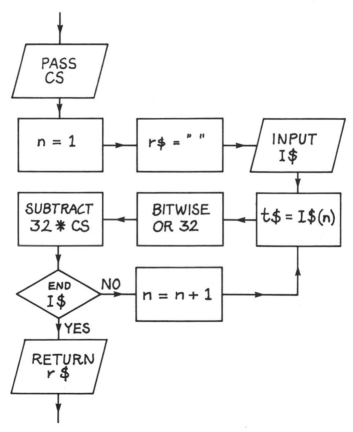

Flowchart 2.2:   GET$ PROCedure.

(Note that all variables used are LOCal to the FuNction and are defined in lower case to distinguish them from global variables.)

As it stands, this will modify *all* characters, which produces problems such as a space (CHR$(32)) being transformed into CHR$(0) which is non-displayable! We can prevent the conversion of spaces and numerals by restricting the modification to characters having certain CODEs. A simple way to do this is to restrict modification to characters having CODEs greater than 65, by multiplying (32*cs) by NOT CODE (t$)<65. Now if the CODE of t$ is less than 65, then (32*cs) will NOT be subtracted, and the character will be unchanged.

```
20070      r$=r$ & CHR$((CODE(t$) || 32)-
           (32*cs) * NOT CODE(t$)<65)
```

Invalid requests

If you type in anything other than the four key 'command words' then nothing will be printed, except for another input request. It would be more user-friendly if the computer indicated more clearly than your command was not valid. You could do that by adding a test that none of the command words has been found, but that becomes very long-winded, and effectively impossible when you have a long list of valid words.

```
11140      IF IN$<>"NORTH" AND IN$<>"SOUTH" AND
           IN$<>"WEST" AND IN$<>"EAST" THEN
11150         CSIZE 1,1 : PRINT "INVALID REQUEST"
              : CSIZE 1,0
11160      END IF
```

On the other hand, adding NEXT DIRECTION to the end of each IF–THEN line will force a direct jump back to the INPUT when a valid command is detected. If all the IF tests are not true then the program falls through to line 11150 which prints a warning. Making direct jumps back when a valid word is found is a good idea anyway, as it saves the system making unnecessary tests when the answer has already been found (see **Flowchart 2.3**).

```
11100      IF IN$="NORTH" THEN PRINT "NORTH" :
           NEXT DIRECTION
11110      IF IN$="SOUTH" THEN PRINT "SOUTH" :
           NEXT DIRECTION
11120      IF IN$="WEST" THEN PRINT "WEST" : NEXT
           DIRECTION
11130      IF IN$="EAST" THEN PRINT "EAST" : NEXT
           DIRECTION
11140      REMark DELETED
11160      REMark DELETED
```

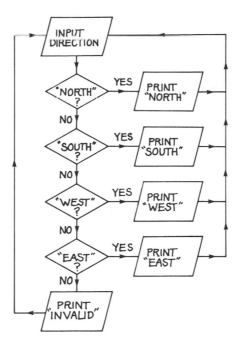

Flowchart 2.3:   Deleting Unnecessary Tests.

Adding some action

That will echo the command given on the screen but of course it does not
actually *do* anything. As a model to work with we will introduce Boris the
turtle, who will move around the screen in response to our commands. To
conveniently display him separately from the text we will divide the
screen up into windows in a SCREEN PROCedure, which splits the
screen vertically with window #1 (white) on the left and #2 (green) on the
right. Now text will appear on the right window, and Boris's trail on the
left window.

```
12000 DEFine PROCedure SCREEN
12010    MODE 4
12020    WINDOW #1,230,200,257,16
12030    BORDER #1,1,2
12040    CSIZE #1,1,0
12050    PAPER #1,4
12060    INK #1,0
12070    CLS #1
12080    WINDOW #2,230,200,26,16
12090    BORDER #2,1,2
```

```
12100    CSIZE #2,1,0
12110    PAPER #2,7
12120    INK #2,0
12130    CLS #2
12140    INK #0,7
12150    CLS #0
12160 END DEFine SCREEN
```

The START PROCedure must now call SCREEN, set an appropriate drawing SCALE, and move the turtle to his start position. The absolute coordinates of the start position are 10,10 in channel #2, but it is simpler if we express movement as plus and minus in relation to this point by means of variables X% and Y%.

```
10010    SCREEN
10020    SCALE #2,20,0,0
10030    LINE #2,10,10
10040    X%=0 : Y%=0
```

The actual screen movement is dealt with by the TRACK PROCedure, which draws a LINE_Relative to the last point (0,0). Notice that the updating parameters are passed to TRACK as X1 and Y1.

```
13000 DEFine PROCedure TRACK(X1,Y1)
13010    LINE_R #2,0,0 TO X1,Y1
13020 END DEFine TRACK
```

We now need to add the real response to your command, as well as the message indicating that it has been understood, and a printout of your current position (see **Flowchart 2.4**).

```
11020        UNDER 0 : PRINT \"DIRECTION?"\"X=";
             X%,"Y=";Y%

11100        IF IN$="NORTH" THEN PRINT "NORTH" :
             Y%=Y%+1 : TRACK 0,1 : NEXT DIRECTION
11110        IF IN$="SOUTH" THEN PRINT "SOUTH" :
             Y%=((Y%*3)-3)/3 : TRACK 0,-1 : NEXT
             DIRECTION
11120        IF IN$="WEST" THEN PRINT "WEST" :
             X%=((X%*3)-3)/3 : TRACK -1,0 : NEXT
             DIRECTION
11130        IF IN$="EAST" THEN PRINT "EAST" :
             X%=X%+1 : TRACK 1,0 : NEXT DIRECTION
```

14

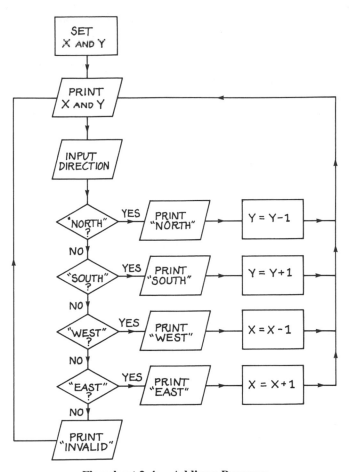

Flowchart 2.4:   Adding a Response.

(You may notice that lines 11110 and 11120 look a little strange as $X\% = ((X\%*3)-3)/3$ and $Y\%=((Y\%*3)-3)/3$ effectively only subtract one from $X\%$ and $Y\%$. The reason for this long-winded path is that the initial version of the QL had a bug which caused $-1-1$, $-2-2$, and $-4-4$ to all result in 0! As -3 is the smallest number which can be subtracted correctly, $X\%$ is multiplied by 3 before subtracting 3 and divided by 3 again! If your machine can successfully calculate $-1-1=-2$ then you can replace this long version with $X\%=X\%-1$ and $Y\%=Y\%-1$, wherever it appears in this book.)

Using direction PROCedures

Of course that is a very simple example and, particularly where the results of your actions are more complicated, it may be better to put the responses into individual PROCedures.

```
11100      IF IN$="NORTH" THEN NORTH : NEXT
           DIRECTION
11110      IF IN$="SOUTH" THEN SOUTH : NEXT
           DIRECTION
11120      IF IN$="WEST" THEN WEST : NEXT
           DIRECTION
11130      IF IN$="EAST" THEN EAST : NEXT
           DIRECTION

14000 DEFine PROCedure NORTH
14010   PRINT "GOING NORTH"
14020   Y%=Y%+1
14030   TRACK 0,1
14090 END DEFine NORTH

14100 DEFine PROCedure SOUTH
14110   PRINT "GOING SOUTH"
14120   Y%=((Y%*3)-3)/3
14130   TRACK 0,-1
14140 END DEFine SOUTH

15000 DEFine PROCedure WEST
15010   PRINT "GOING WEST"
15020   X%=((X%*3)-3)/3
15030   TRACK -1,0
15040 END DEFine WEST

16000 DEFine PROCedure EAST
16010   PRINT "GOING EAST"
16020   X%=X%+1
16030   TRACK 1,0
16040 END DEFine EAST
```

More versatility

You could extend this use of IF–THEN tests ad infinitum (or rather ad memoriam finitum!) but it is really rather a crude way of doing things which creates problems when you want to make your programs more sophisticated. A more versatile way to deal with command words and responses is to enter them as DATA and then store them in string arrays.

First you must DIMension arrays of suitable length for command words, C$, and responses, R$. As only fixed length string arrays are allowed in SuperBASIC, both the length of each element (20), and the number of elements (3) must be defined. (Note that SuperBASIC has a zero element which is also used, thus catering for the four directions.) We now also need to think about how we will match these array elements against the INPUT. The length of an ordinary string input will be the number of characters entered — but the length of the array elements is fixed at 20, with any unused positions being filled with CHR$(0).

Now an input of:

NORTH

cannot be equal to an array element containing

NORTH (plus 15 empty positions)

unless we force our INPUT string into the same format by declaring it with a DIM (IN$,20) statement.

```
10050    DIM C$(3,20),R$(3,20),IN$(20)
```

If you put the commands and responses in pairs in the DATA statement then it is more difficult to get them jumbled up and easier to read them in turn into the equivalent element in each array (see **Table 2.2**).

Table 2.2:   Content of Command and Response Arrays.

ELEMENT NUMBER	COMMAND WORD (C$(n))	RESPONSE (R$(n))
0	NORTH	GOING NORTH
1	SOUTH	GOING SOUTH
2	WEST	GOING WEST
3	EAST	GOING EAST

At this point we will add some lines to the START PROCedure which will initialise the arrays (fill them with your words). As SuperBASIC does not automatically RESTORE on RUN, this must be done explicitly.

```
10060    RESTORE
10100    DATA "NORTH","GOING NORTH","SOUTH",
         "GOING SOUTH","WEST","GOING WEST",
         "EAST","GOING EAST"
10200    FOR N=0 TO 3
```

```
10210      READ C$(N) : READ R$(N)
10220    END FOR N
```

All those IF–THEN tests can be replaced by a single loop which compares your INPUT with each element of the array containing the command words (C$) in turn (see **Flowchart 2.5**).

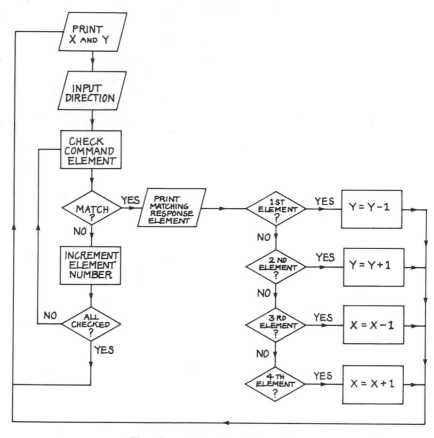

Flowchart 2.5:   More Versatility.

```
11100    FOR N=0 TO 3
11110      IF IN$<>C$(N) THEN
11120    END FOR N
11130    REMark DELETED
11140    REMark DELETED
11160       ELSE
11170          PRINT R$(N)

11200       END IF
```

Now IF your INPUT does not match any of the command words the test falls through, or ELSE the corresponding response element (R$(N)) is printed out.

Of course we are now back in our original position of actually doing nothing, so we need to add back some actions. We will do this through a new POSITION PROCedure which is called when a match is found.   •

11180   POSITION

We still have a pointer to indicate which word matched the input as N (the number of array elements checked) holds this value. POSITION uses this in the SELect command to move to appropriate routines which are similar to those we wrote earlier, except that there is no need to define the particular message, as this has already been printed as R$(N).

```
14000 DEFine PROCedure POSITION
14010    SELect ON N
14020       ON N=0
14030          Y%=Y%+1
14040          TRACK 0,1
14100       ON N=1
14110          Y%=((Y%*3)-3)/3
14120          TRACK 0,-1
14140    REMark DELETED
14190    REMark DELETED
14200       ON N=2
14210          X%=((X%*3)-3)/3
14220          TRACK -1,0
14230    REMark DELETED
14290    REMark DELETED
14300       ON N=3
14310          X%=X%+1
14320          TRACK 1,0
14330    END SELect
14390 END DEFine POSITION
```

Expanding the vocabulary

The arrays can easily be expanded to contain more words and it would be better if we defined the number of words as a variable, WD%, which we would then use to DIMension the arrays and for both the filling and scanning loops. This produces a general routine which is easily modified.

```
10050     WD%=3 : DIM C$(WD%,20),R$(WD%,20),
          IN$(20)

10200     FOR N=0 TO WD%

11100       FOR N=0 TO WD%
```

For example we can add intermediate compass directions which change both X and Y axes.

```
10050     WD%=7 : DIM C$(WD%,20),R$(WD%,20),
          IN$(20)
10110     DATA "NORTH EAST","GOING NORTH EAST"
          ,"SOUTH EAST","GOING SOUTH EAST"
10120     DATA "SOUTH WEST","GOING SOUTH WEST"
          ,"NORTH WEST","GOING NORTH WEST"
```

and add some more actions:

```
14330     REMark DELETED
14390     REMark DELETED
14400       ON N=4
14410         Y%=Y%+1 : X%=X%+1
14420         TRACK 1,1
14500       ON N=5
14510         Y%=((Y%*3)-3)/3 : X%=X%+1
14520         TRACK 1,-1
14600       ON N=6
14610         Y%=((Y%*3)-3)/3 : X%=((X%*3)-3)/3
14620         TRACK -1,-1
14700       ON N=7
14710         Y%=Y%+1 : X%=((X%*3)-3)/3
14720         TRACK -1,1
14730     END SELect
14740 END DEFine POSITION
```

Removing redundancy

All the responses so far have included the word 'GOING' and this word has actually been typed into each DATA statement. Now typing practice is very good for the soul but it would be much more sensible to define this common word as a string variable. Notice that a space is included at the end to space it from the following word. All occurrences of the word 'GOING' can be deleted from the DATA and G$ combined with each key word in the response instead.

```
10100    DATA "NORTH","NORTH","SOUTH","SOUTH",
         "WEST","WEST","EAST","EAST"
10110    DATA "NORTH EAST","NORTH EAST","SOUTH
         EAST","SOUTH EAST"
10120    DATA "SOUTH WEST","SOUTH WEST","NORTH
         WEST","NORTH WEST"

10130     G$="GOING "

11170     PRINT G$;R$(N)
```

Now that is starting to look rather silly as both arrays contain exactly the same words, so why not get rid of the response arrays, R$, and simply print C$(N)? Well, in this case you could do that without any problem, but of course where the responses are not simply a repetition of the input (as is very often the case) the second array is essential.

If you look hard at all those action PROCedures you will realise that they all do essentially one thing — update the values of X% and Y%. Now we could include that information in the original DATA and get rid of them altogether! We need to add two more arrays to hold the X and Y coordinates, add the appropriate values into the DATA lines after each response, and READ in the information in blocks of four (INPUT, RESPONSE, X-MOVE, Y-MOVE — see **Table 2.3**).

Table 2.3:   X and Y Moves Incorporated into Arrays.

ELEMENT NUMBER	COMMAND WORD C$(n)	RESPONSE R$(n)	X-MOVE X(n)	Y-MOVE Y(n)
1	NORTH	NORTH	0	-1
2	SOUTH	SOUTH	0	1
3	WEST	WEST	-1	0
4	EAST	EAST	1	0
5	NORTH-EAST	NORTH-EAST	1	-1
6	SOUTH-EAST	SOUTH-EAST	1	1
7	SOUTH-WEST	SOUTH-WEST	-1	1
8	NORTH-WEST	NORTH-WEST	-1	-1

```
10050    WD%=7 : DIM C$(WD%,20),R$(WD%,20),IN$
         (20),X(WD%),Y(WD%)

10100    DATA "NORTH","NORTH"0,1,"SOUTH",
         "SOUTH",0,-1,"WEST","WEST",-1,0,
         "EAST","EAST",1,0
```

```
10110    DATA "NORTH EAST","NORTH EAST",1,1,
         "SOUTH EAST","SOUTH EAST",1,-1
10120    DATA "SOUTH WEST","SOUTH WEST",-1,-1
         ,"NORTH WEST","NORTH WEST",-1,1

10210    READ C$(N) : READ R$(N) : READ X(N)
         : READ Y(N)
```

Now we can delete all the redundant lines and modify the TRACK PROCedure so that X% and Y% are suitably updated (see **Flowchart 2.6**).

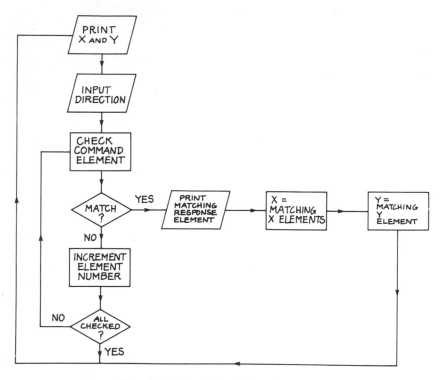

Flowchart 2.6:   Using Linked Arrays.

```
14010    X%=((X%*3)+(X(N)*3))/3 :
         Y%=((Y%*3)+(Y(N)*3))/3
14020    TRACK X(N),Y(N)

14030    REMark DLINE 14030 TO 14730
```

This overall pattern of putting all the information into a series of linked arrays is a very common feature which is used in several of the later programs in this book.

Abbreviated commands

So far we have always used complete words as commands, but that means that you have to do a lot of typing to give the machine your instructions. If you are feeling lazy, you might think of changing the command words to the first letter of the word only, and then INPUT a single letter. However, unless you start using random letters, that will only start work as long as no two words start with the same letter! To code all the eight compass directions used above, we will have to use up two letters: N, NE, E, SE, S, SW, W, NW.

```
10100    DATA "N","NORTH",0,1,"S","SOUTH",0,-
         1,"W","WEST",-1,0,"E","EAST",1,0
10110    DATA "NE","NORTH EAST",1,1,"SE",
         "SOUTH EAST",1,-1
10120    DATA "SW","SOUTH WEST",-1,-1,"NW",
         "NORTH WEST",-1,1
```

Notice that it is only the actual command words which have changed and that the computer gives a full description of the direction, as we are still using that second array which holds the response.

Partial matching

In all the programs above we have always checked that the input matched a word in the command array *exactly*. However it would be useful if we could allow a number of similar words to be acceptable as meaning the same thing. For example, you could check whether the first letter of the input word matched the abbreviated keyword by only comparing the first character (taking IN$(1)).

```
11080      IN$=IN$(1)
```

That will work with NORTH, SOUTH, EAST and WEST, but there are obvious problems in dealing with the intermediate positions, so we will get rid of these positions again.

```
10050    WD%=3 : DIM C$(WD%,20),R$(WD%,20),
         IN$(20),X(WD%),Y(WD%)
10110    REMark DELETED
10120    REMark DELETED
```

In addition there are lots of words beginning with the letters N, S, E and W — all of which would be equally acceptable to the machine as a valid direction.

For example:

NOT NORTH

would produce:

GOING NORTH

A more selective process is to match a number of letters instead of just one. In this example, the first three letters of the four main directions are quite characteristic.

NOR
SOU
EAS
WES

If you use these as command words then, for example:

NOR
NORTH
NORTHERN
and NORTHERLY

will all be equally acceptable, but:

NOT
NEARLY
NOWHERE
and NONSENSE

will all be rejected.

All we need to do is to take the first three letters of the input, IN$(1 TO 3), and compare them with a revised DATA list.

```
10100    DATA "NOR","NORTH",0,1,"SOU","SOUTH"
         ,0,-1,"WES","WEST",-1,0,"EAS","EAST"
         ,1,0

11080      IN$=IN$(1 TO 3)
```

Sequential commands

In the routines above we have dealt with the intermediate compass positions as separate entities, but if we could give a sequence of commands at the same time we would not need to do this. There is always more than one way to get to any point and if more than one command word could be understood at the same time we would not have to worry about checking for directions such as 'NORTH EAST' as they could be dealt with by the combination of 'NORTH' and 'EAST'.

This brings us to the very significant question of how to split an input into words. First you must ask yourself how you recognise that a series of characters make up a separate word? The answer, of course, is that you see a *space* between them. Now, if we look for spaces we can break the input into separate words which we can look at individually. The easiest way to look for spaces is with the INSTR command which searches the whole of a designated search string for a match with a second target string.

To begin with we will incorporate INSTR into a WORDSPLIT FuNction which is now called from line 11080.

```
11080     WORDSPLIT

15000 DEFine FuNction WORDSPLIT
15010   SP%=" " INSTR IN$
15030   PRINT "SP% ";SP%
15090 END DEFine WORDSPLIT
```

This starts by checking whether the first character in IN$ is a space. If it is not a space, then it will automatically continue checking until the end of IN$ is reached. If no space is found in the whole of IN$ then SP% will be set to zero. If a space is found the value of SP% will be the number of characters along IN$ that the space is located (see **Flowchart 2.7**). The temporary line 15030 prints out SP% so that you can observe INSTR in action.

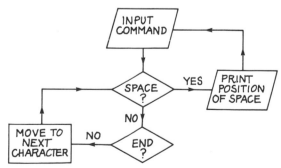

Flowchart 2.7:   Locating the Position of a Space.

25

Try this out with:

NOR WES

SP% 4

NORTH WEST

SP% 6

NOR NOR WEST

SP% 4

(Note that you will also get an 'Invalid request' message for the moment as IN$ is no longer converted to the first three characters only.)

Although the length of the word is accounted for by SP%, only the first space is found. To find all the spaces we are going to have to work harder.

First of all a space needs to be added to the front end of IN$, so that the first word has the same format as the others, and we must define the start position of the search (ST%) as zero.

```
11080      IN$=" " & IN$ : ST%=0
11090      WORDSPLIT
```

The WORDSPLIT FuNction is now modified to find and cut out each word in the INPUT (see **Flowchart 2.8**). Once a space has been found (at SP%) a new search start position is defined as one character further along IN$ (at ST%), a word (W$) cut out as the first three characters following the space (ST% TO ST%+2), and the INPUT string (IN$) truncated so that it only contains the unchecked part of the entry (IN$(ST% TO)).

```
15010   SP%=" " INSTR IN$
```

```
15030   ST%=SP%+1
```

```
15070   W$=IN$(ST% TO ST%+2) : IN$=IN$(ST% TO)
```

As WORDSPLIT was DEFined as a FuNction, we can use it to return different values. We will RETurn minus one if no space is found (SP%=0), and zero if a space is found and a word cut out.

```
15020      IF SP%=0 THEN RETurn -1
```

```
15080   RETurn 0
```

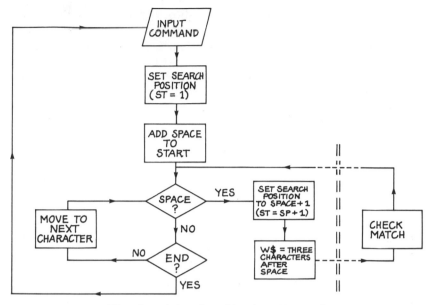

Flowchart 2.8:   Searching for a Keyword.

Now we can use the value RETurned by WORDSPLIT to EXIT the
REPeat WORDS loop as soon as no word is found.

11090   IF WORDSPLIT THEN EXIT WORDS

Now typing:

NORTH WEST

produces:

GOING NORTH
GOING WEST

and even:

NOR NOR EAST

is decoded as:

GOING NORTH

GOING NORTH

GOING EAST

It would be a lot neater if we deleted all those redundant 'GOINGs' and put all the reported directions on the same line. We need to PRINT G$ once, immediately before the INSTR check. Now each time we go through the loop comparing the current word with those stored, we 'PRINT R$(N);' if there is a match. As there is a semicolon after this the words will be printed on the same line but we also need to add spaces between them.

```
11080      IN$=" " & IN$ : ST%=0 : PRINT G$;

11170          PRINT R$(N);" ";
```

Now:

NORTH EASTERLY SOUTH WEST

sends you neatly round in circles

GOING NORTH EAST SOUTH WEST

CHAPTER 3
Understanding Natural Language

So far we have only communicated with the computer in a very restricted way as it has only been programmed to understand a very few words or letters and it only recognises those if they are entered in exactly the right way. For example, if you put a space before or after your command as you INPUT it then it will be rejected. This is because we are comparing whether the two strings match exactly.

However, in the real world everyone uses what is known as natural language, which is a very sophisticated and extremely variable thing which only the human brain can cope with effectively. Even if we forget for the moment the differences between 'English' and 'American' or even regional dialects of either of those (can 'Ow bist old but' really mean 'How are you old friend'?), dealing with language has an infinite number of problems.

Even the most sophisticated systems in the world cannot cope with everything. There is an old story which illustrates this point very well. The CIA developed a superb translation program which could instantly convert English into Russian and vice versa. In the hope of impressing the President they laid on a demonstration of its capabilities in which it converted everything he said into Russian, spoke that, and then retranslated the Russian back into English. He was most impressed and was totally absorbed until one of his aides reminded him that he had forgotten that the First Lady was waiting for him outside. When he ruefully commented 'out of sight, out of mind' he was amazed to hear the machine come back with 'invisible maniac'!

Dealing with sentences

Everyone knows that real language is made up of sentences, but what exactly do we mean by a sentence? Well, the most obvious way we recognise a sentence is that we see a full stop! However, if we are going to be able to deal with sentences we are going to have to think a lot harder than that.

The Oxford Dictionary definition includes 'a series of words in connected speech or writing, forming grammatically complete expression of single thought, and usually containing subject and predicate, and conveying statement, question, command or request' but also concedes that it is used loosely to mean 'part of writing or speech between two full stops'. Phew! Can somebody translate that into everyday English, please? The intricacies and illogicalities of the English language are infamous, so how can we expect a computer to cope?

Parsing the parcel

Before we can understand a sentence we must break it down into its component parts before we can analyse the significance of each individual segment. This process of dividing up the sentence is known as 'parsing' by the cognoscenti, so there's one more piece of jargon to impress your friends if you are that way inclined.

Let's start by looking at some simple examples of sentences.

I WANT.

consists of a subject I and a verb WANT.

I WANT BISCUITS.

also has an object BISCUITS.

I WANT CHOCOLATE BISCUITS.

qualifies the object with an adjective CHOCOLATE.

I SOMETIMES WANT CHOCOLATE BISCUITS.

qualifies the verb with an adverb SOMETIMES.

The most important word in all the above examples was 'WANT', as it conveyed the main idea. The second example was more informative as it indicated that only one particular type of object, BISCUITS, was wanted. The addition of an adjective, CHOCOLATE, gave further information on the type of object wanted, but life became more uncertain again when the adverb SOMETIMES was included.

Now how could a computer program decode such sentences? The answer must be to find some logical structure in the sentence, so what 'rules' could we lay down for this example?

1) All started with a subject, I, and ended with a full stop.
2) The last word was always the object BISCUITS (unless there was no object and only two words).

3) If the word before the object was not the verb WANT, it was an adjective, CHOCOLATE.

4) If the word before the verb was not the subject, I, it was an adverb, SOMETIMES.

Let's write a program in which we give the computer sentences and ask it to break them up into their component parts.

To begin with, we will set up a suitable SCREEN format with three windows. Channel #0 at the bottom receives your input, and the rest of the screen is split horizontally into windows #1 and #2. Window #1 (lower) shows the final results of the program, whilst window #2 (upper) displays the workings of certain subroutines.

```
30 SCREEN
```

```
10000 DEFine PROCedure SCREEN
10010    MODE 4
10020    CLS
10030    WINDOW #0,435,40,36,216
10040    WINDOW #1,455,100,26,116
10050    WINDOW #2,455,100,26,16
10060    BORDER #0,5,4
10070    BORDER #1,3,2
10080    BORDER #2,3,2
10090    PAPER #0,0
10100    PAPER #1,7
10110    PAPER #2,4
10120    INK #0,7
10130    INK #1,0
10140    INK #2,0
10150    CSIZE #0,1,0
10160    CSIZE #1,1,0
10170    CSIZE #2,1,0
10180    CLS #0 : CLS #1 : CLS #2
10190 END DEFine SCREEN
```

We need to give it a vocabulary of objects, adjectives and adverbs to work with, by calling a SET_UP PROCedure which READs these from DATA and stores them in arrays OB$(n,10), AJ$(n,10) and AV$(n,10), according to type. Note that the length of the longest word (10) must be taken into account when DIMensioning the arrays and that the number of each type of word is defined as a variable (OB%, AJ%, AV%) so that it is easy to add more words later.

```
  10 RESTORE
  40 SET_UP

11000 DEFine PROCedure SET_UP
11010    OB%=5 : AJ%=5 : AV%=2 : DIM OB$(OB%,10)
         ,AJ$(AJ%,10),AV$(AV%,10)
11020    DATA "BISCUITS","BUNS","CAKE","COFFEE"
         ,"TEA","WATER"
11030    DATA "CHOCOLATE","GINGER","JAM","COLD"
         ,"HOT","LUKEWARM"
11040    DATA "ALWAYS","OFTEN","SOMETIMES"
11050      FOR N=0 TO OB%
11060        READ OB$(N)
11070      END FOR N
11080      FOR N=0 TO AJ%
11090        READ AJ$(N)
11100      END FOR N
11110      FOR N=0 TO AV%
11120        READ AV$(N)
11130      END FOR N
11140 END DEFine SET_UP
```

Now we need to INPUT the sentence to be parsed, using the GET\$(1) FuNction described previously, and a REPeat IN loop. (Don't forget that you can use MERGE to transfer the original GET\$ lines from the program described in the last chapter!)

The sentence must be broken into words (see **Flowchart 3.1**). To make life easier, we will add a space on to the end of IN\$, so that the format of the last word looks just like that of other words, and also a dummy character (*) right at the end for reasons which are explained below.

```
120      IN$=IN$ & " *"
```

Once again we will use an INSTR search for spaces, and then cut out and store each word. This is done here with the REPeat WORDS loop and the WORDSTORE FuNction. The initial search start is defined as ST% = 1.

```
130      ST%=1
170      REPeat WORDS
180        IF WORDSTORE THEN EXIT WORDS
190      END REPeat WORDS
```

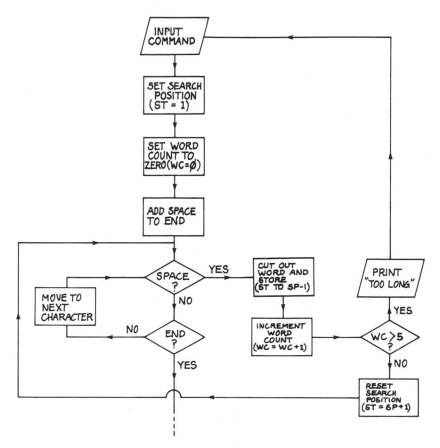

Flowchart 3.1:   Cutting Out Words.

If a space is not found (SP% = 0) then the end of the sentence has been reached, and WORDSTORE RETurns a value of −1. If WORDSTORE RETurns any value other than zero then we EXIT the WORDS loop.

```
12000 DEFine FuNction WORDSTORE

12020    SP%=" " INSTR IN$
12030      IF SP%=0 THEN RETurn −1

12090 END DEFine WORDSTORE
```

If a space is found, the section of IN$ from ST% (current search start) to SP%−1 (current space−1 = length of word) is cut out, the word count (WC%) incremented, and the section stored in a word store array, W$(WC%).

```
  20 DIM W$(5,10)

  60 WC%=-1

12040    WC%=WC%+1

12060    W$(WC%)=IN$(ST% TO SP%-1)
```

To begin with, ST% = 1 so that the search starts at the first character in the input string, and the word count variable, WC%, is set to zero (ie −1 +1) so that the first word found is stored in the zero element of the word store array. The word count is incremented in each cycle so that the next element of the array W$ is used next time.

The length of IN$ is now reduced by cutting off the word already stored from the front end to leave IN$(SP%+1 TO) and a value of 0 RETurned by the FuNction. As WORDSTORE is therefore zero, the WORDS loop is repeated. The dummy asterisk at the end is needed as the new IN$ is always defined as one more than the last space, so that the ultimate end of IN$ must *not* be a space.

```
12070    IN$=IN$(SP%+1 TO)
12080    RETurn 0
```

Adding the following lines will produce a printout in the upper window showing the reducing length of IN$ as the search proceeds.

```
  150    UNDER #2, 1 : PRINT #2,"IN$"\ :
         UNDER #2, 0

12010    PRINT#2,, IN$
```

A check is made that there are not more than six (0 to 5) words in the sentence, as that would exceed the array size. If this is true then WC% is reset to −1, and WORDSTORE RETurns −1, so that we EXIT the WORDS loop.

```
12050    IF WC%>5 THEN PRINT "SENTENCE TOO
         LONG" : WC%=-1 : RETurn -1
```

When the search is completed (END REPeat WORDS), the list of words found is printed out in the lower window.

```
160       UNDER #1, 1 : PRINT #1,"W$(N)"\ :
          UNDER #1, 0

200       FOR N=0 TO WC%
210         PRINT, W$(N);" "
220       END FOR N
```

A test is now made to see whether there is a match between words in the sentence W$(N) and the objects in the vocabulary array OB$(N) (see **Flowchart 3.2**). Only words 2, 3 and 4 are checked as these are the only possible positions for the object in our restricted sentence format. Three different PROCedures are jumped to according to the position of the matching word in the sentence. If no match is found a message is printed and a new input requested.

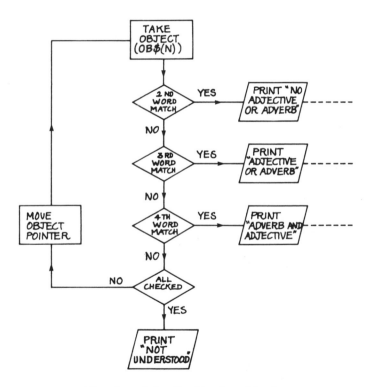

Flowchart 3.2:   Looking for a Match.

```
230       FOR N=0 TO OB%
240         IF W$(2)=OB$(N) THEN NEITHER :
          NEXT IN
```

```
250          IF W$(3)=OB$(N) THEN EITHER :
             NEXT IN
260          IF W$(4)=OB$(N) THEN BOTH :
             NEXT IN
270       END FOR N
280     PRINT \,"object not found"
290   END REPeat IN
```

If the object was found as word 3, then there was *neither* adjective nor adverb.

```
1000 DEFine PROCedure NEITHER
1010   PRINT \,"no adjective or adverb"
1020 END DEFine NEITHER
```

If the object was found as word 4, there could have been *either* an adjective or an adverb in the sentence (see **Flowchart 3.3**).

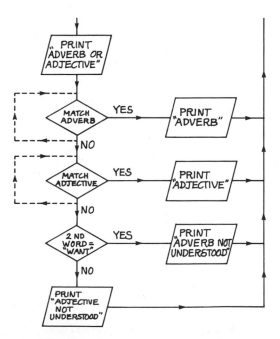

Flowchart 3.3:   Adverb or Adjective.

```
2000 DEFine PROCedure EITHER
2010   PRINT \,"either adjective or adverb"
```

First we check for a match between the second word and the contents of the adverb array.

```
2020      FOR N=0 TO AV%
2030        IF W$(1)=AV$(N) THEN PRINT ,
            "ADVERB" : RETurn
2040      END FOR N
```

If no match is found then we check the third word against the adjective list.

```
2050      FOR N=0 TO AJ%
2060        IF W$(2)=AJ$(N) THEN PRINT ,
            "ADJECTIVE" : RETurn
2070      END FOR N
```

If a match is not found in either of these lists, then it would be useful to indicate which word was not understood. The simplest answer is to check whether the second word was not the verb 'WANT', as in that case the second word must have been an adverb. On the other hand if the second word was the verb then the third word must have been an adjective. Notice that the actual word which did not match is now included in the message.

```
2080      IF W$(1) <>"WANT" THEN PRINT \
          "ADVERB ";W$(1);" NOT UNDERSTOOD" :
          RETurn
2090      PRINT \"ADJECTIVE ";W$(2);" NOT
          UNDERSTOOD" : RETurn

2100 END DEFine EITHER
```

If a match is found in any test then we RETurn. Note that these possibilities are exclusive and that in four words we can only have one or the other.

Where *both* adverb and adjective are present we must check for both (with ADV_CHECK and ADJ_CHECK), and therefore a match in the first test also jumps on to the second test (see **Flowchart 3.4**).

```
3000 DEFine PROCedure BOTH
3010   PRINT \"ADVERB and ADJECTIVE"
3020   ADV_CHECK
3030   ADJ_CHECK
3040 END DEFine BOTH
```

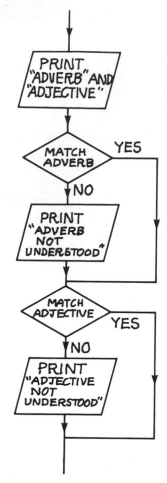

Flowchart 3.4:   Adverb and Adjective.

If an ADVerb is found then we RETurn to the *last* PROCedure (ie BOTH) and continue with ADJ_CHECK. Otherwise the word not recognised is reported before ADJ_CHECK is called.

```
4000 DEFine PROCedure ADV_CHECK
4010    FOR N=0 TO AV%
4020       IF W$(1)=AV$(N) THEN RETurn
4030    END FOR N
4040    PRINT "adverb ";W$(1);" not understood"
4050 END DEFine ADV_CHECK
```

ADJ_CHECK works in the same way.

```
5000 DEFine PROCedure ADJ_CHECK
5010   FOR N=0 TO AJ%
5020     IF W$(3)=AJ$(N) THEN RETurn
5030   NEXT N
5040   PRINT "adjective ";W$(3);" not
       understood"
5050 END DEFine ADJ_CHECK
```

What about punctuation?

As we already said, you usually recognise the end of a sentence because it has a full stop, although when you type into a computer you usually forget all about such trivialities. But what will happen in the program so far if some 'clever' user puts in the correct punctuation? If you think for a moment you will realise that the computer will start complaining as it will no longer recognise the last word, as this will actually be split out as the word *plus* the full stop.

We therefore need to check if the last character in the input string IN$ is a full stop. The best place to check PUNCTUATION seems to be immediately after the INPUT. If the end character (EN$ = IN$ (LEN(IN$))) is a full stop then simply CHOP this character off and then RETurn.

```
90      PUNCTUATION

6000 DEFine PROCedure PUNCTUATION
6010   EN$=IN$(LEN(IN$))
6020     IF EN$="." THEN CHOP : RETurn
6050 END DEFine PUNCTUATION

7000 DEFine PROCedure CHOP
7010   IN$=IN$(1 TO LEN(IN$)-1)
7020 END DEFine CHOP
```

Other punctuation marks may also appear at the end of the sentence so perhaps we should look closer at the last character. More useful sentence terminators are the question and exclamation marks which often indicate the context of the words.

```
6030      IF EN$="?" THEN CHOP : PRINT #0,"
          QUESTION?"\
6040      IF EN$="!" THEN CHOP : PRINT #0,"
          EXCLAMATION"\
```

In many dialects of BASIC, the INPUT command will not accept anything after a comma, which it reads as data terminator, but fortunately SuperBASIC has no objections. Commas may be useful in indicating different parts of a sentence, which could be examined as 'sub-sentences' in their own right. However, in simple cases they are best deleted and replaced by spaces before the sentence is broken into words (see **Flowchart 3.5**). Note that this will only function totally correctly if there is no space after the comma, as any space following a replaced comma will be seen as a new word. If no comma is found (CM% = 0) then we RETurn, otherwise the lefthand part of IN$ (up to the comma), and the righthand part of IN$ (beyond the comma) are taken and joined together with a space.

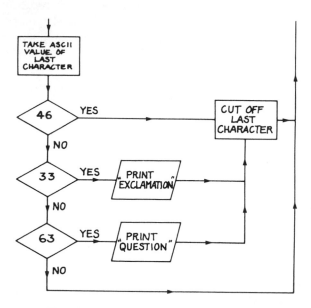

Flowchart 3.5: Dealing with Punctuation.

```
  100     COMMA

 8000 DEFine PROCedure COMMA
 8010    REPeat comloop
 8020       CM%="," INSTR IN$
 8030          IF CM%=0 THEN RETurn
 8040          IN$=IN$(1 TO CM%-1) & " " & IN$(CM%+1
               TO )
 8050    END REPeat comloop
 8060 END DEFine COMMA
```

Apostrophes can be dealt with in the same way, except that we do not replace them with a space but simply close up the words.

```
   110      APOSTROPHE


9000 DEFine PROCedure APOSTROPHE
9010   REPeat aposloop
9020     AP%="'" INSTR IN$
9030       IF AP%=0 THEN RETurn
9040       IN$=IN$(1 TO AP%-1) & IN$(AP%+1 TO )
9050     END REPeat aposloop
9060 END DEFine APOSTROPHE
```

A sliding search approach

Although the method of examining a sentence described above will work it has the disadvantage that it requires the sentence to be entered in a particular restricted format. For example if you enter:

I WANT REALLY HOT CHOCOLATE CAKE

the computer will report:

OBJECT NOT FOUND

as it only looks for objects as far as the fifth word.

Using a sliding search of the whole sentence for each keyword, without first dividing the sentence down into words, has the advantage that it allows a completely free input format. In this approach we take the first keyword and try to match it against the same number of letters in IN$, starting at the first character. If this test fails then it is automatically repeated, starting from the second character, etc, until a match is found or the end of IN$ is reached. For example if IN$ was 'I WANT CAKE' and the first keyword was 'CAKE', the comparisons would be:

pass 1	I	W	A	
pass 2		W	A	N
pass 3	W	A	N	T
pass 4	A	N	T	
pass 5	N	T		C
pass 6	T		C	A
pass 7		C	A	K
pass 8	C	A	K	E	(match found)

We can use much of our existing program, but substantial changes are also required. Therefore delete all the lines from 80 up to 9999 with 'DLINE 80 TO 9999' as a direct command and modify the DIM statement in line 20 to expand the size of the wordstore array (W$(N)) to twenty words. The WORDSTORE FuNction will not be used here so you can also remove that with 'DLINE 12000 TO 12090'.

```
10 RESTORE
20 DIM W$(19,10)
30 SCREEN
40 SET_UP
50   REPeat IN
60     WC%=-1
70     AT #0, 1,1 : IN$=GET$(1)
90     CLS #1 : CLS #2
```

To replace the WORDSTORE FuNction we have a somewhat similar FIND(T$) PROCedure (see **Flowchart 3.6**). This searches IN$ for the temporary string (T$) which is passed to it as a parameter. As T$ is passed when FIND is called, it can be used to perform an INSTR check for any particular string. If no match is found we RETurn. To report what has been found, and so that we can use the words discovered later, we will store each matched word (T$) in an array as it is detected. We have already expanded the word store array, W$, to hold up to 20 words (which should be enough for even a very verbose sentence!).

```
1000 DEFine PROCedure FIND(T$)
1010   IN%=T$ INSTR IN$
1020     IF IN%=0 THEN RETurn
1040   WC%=WC%+1
1050   W$(WC%)=T$
1080   PRINT #2,,,T$
1090 END DEFine FIND
```

Each object can be compared with IN$ by forming a loop, and similar checks can be made for matching with words in the adverb and adjective arrays.

```
120        FOR M=0 TO OB%
130          FIND(OB$(M))
140        END FOR M
150        FOR M=0 TO AV%
160          FIND(AV$(M))
170        END FOR M
```

```
180        FOR M=0 TO AJ%
190          FIND(AJ$(M))
200        END FOR M
```

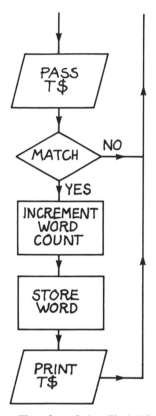

Flowchart 3.6:   Find (T$).

The program waits until the time delay (500) runs out, or a key is pressed, before clearing out the INPUT window and REPeating the request for a sentence.

```
250        DUMMY$=INKEY$(500)
260        CLS #0
270     END REPeat IN
```

Partial matching
One advantage of the sliding search is that you can easily arrange to recognise a series of connected words by only looking for some key

characters. This is obviously useful as it saves you having to put both single and plural nouns such as BISCUIT and BISCUITS. If you amend the DATA in line 11020 as below then both will now be recognised.

```
11020    DATA "BISCUIT","BUN","CAKE","COFFEE"
         ,"TEA","WATER"
```

However life is not that simple, as using BUN rather than BUNS can produce some unexpected results. On the plus side it will detect BUN, BUNS, and BUNFIGHT but unfortunately BUNCH, BUNDLE, BUNGALOW, BUNGLE, BUNK, BUNION, and BUNNY as well!

This problem is not restricted to prefixes as the computer will also not distinguish between HOT and SHOT. You could include a check that the character before the start of each match was a space (ie that this was the start of a word, see **Flowchart 3.7**). IN% gives the current start of word position, so IN$(IN%−1) is the character before this, and we RETurn if this is a space.

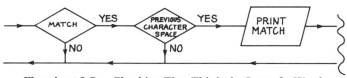

Flowchart 3.7:   Checking That This is the Start of a Word.

```
1030     IF IN$(IN%-1)<>" " THEN RETurn
```

For this to function correctly on the first word, we must add a space to the start of IN$.

```
80       IN$=" " & IN$
```

In a similar way you could use checks on the next letter after the match, or the length of the word, to restrict recognised words.

Putting things in order

Although we have now detected all the words in the sentence, regardless of their position or what else is present, they are found and stored in the order in which they appear in the DATA. This is because the comparison starts with the first item in the object array rather than the first word in the sentence. It would be useful if we could rearrange the wordstore array so that the words in it were in the order in which they appeared in the sentence.

To do that we must keep a record of the sentence position of the word, IN%, and word count, WC%, as each word is matched in a new word position array, WP%. This is a two-dimensional array with the sentence position kept in the first element, WP(WC%,0), and the word count, WP(WC%,1), in the second. To make the display clearer, 'word' and 'position' (ie character position of start of the match in IN$) labels have been added.

```
20 DIM W$(19,10) : DIM WP(19,1)

110     PRINT ,"word","position"

1060   WP(WC%,0)=IN% : WP(WC%,1)=WC%
1070   PRINT #2,,WP(WC%,1),WP(WC%,0);
```

The actual sorting routine which does the rearrangement is in the ORDER PROCedure which is only reached if a match is found.

```
210     ORDER
```

The SORT loop performs a simple exchange sort (see **Flowchart 3.8**). It takes the sentence position (IS%) of the first word found (first element in the first dimension, WP(0,0)) and compares it with the sentence position (IS%) of the second word found (second element in the first dimension, WP(0+1,0)). If the position variable for the first word is of higher value than that for the second word then the first word found is farther along the sentence than the second word, and these therefore need to be exchanged by swapping through a dummy variable (D%). This will put the sentence position pointers right, but the word count markers also need to be rearranged to the correct positions. This process is repeated until the word pointers are all in the correct order. Notice that the actual contents of the string array which holds the words are not altered but only the pointers (index) to them.

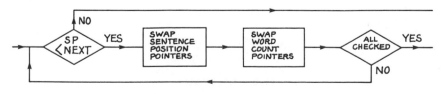

Flowchart 3.8:   Putting Words in Order.

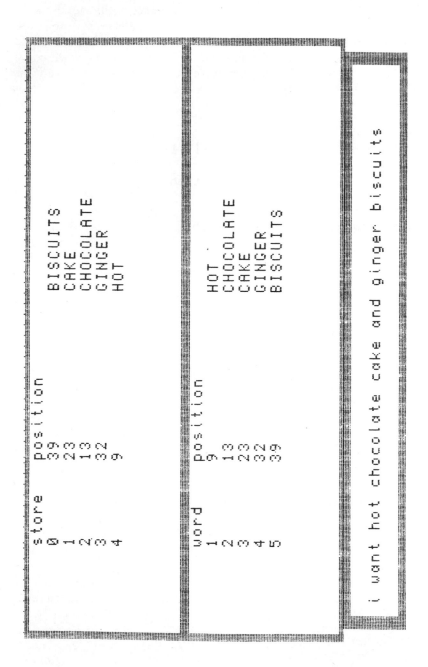

Figure 3.1: Sort.

```
100       PRINT #2,,"store","position"

2000 DEFine PROCedure ORDER
2010   REPeat SORT
2020     FOR N=0 TO WC%-1
2030       IF WP(N,0)>=WP(N+1,0) THEN
2040           D%=WP(N,0) : WP(N,0)=WP(N+1,0) :
                 WP(N+1,0)=D%
2050           D%=WP(N,1) : WP(N,1)=WP(N+1,1) :
                 WP(N+1,1)=D%
2060   END REPeat SORT
2070       END IF
2080     END FOR N
2090 END DEFine ORDER
```

If the strings are now printed in revised word count, WC%, order they will be as they were in the original sentence, which should make it easier to understand them.

```
220       FOR N=0 TO WC%
230         PRINT ,N+1,WP(N,0),,W$(WP(N,1))
240       END FOR N
```

If you RUN some test sentences you will be able to see the original position of the words in the store (top window) and the words then rearranged as in the sentence in the bottom window (see **Figure 3.1**).

Chapter 4
Making Reply

More sensible replies

We have considered at length how to decode sentences which are typed
into the computer, but the replies it has produced so far have been very
limited and rigid. Although many of the original words in a sentence are
often used in a reply, in a real conversation we look at the subject of the
sentence and modify this word according to the context of the reply.

For example the input:

I NEED REST

might expect the confirmatory reply:

YOU NEED REST

and similarly:

YOU NEED REST

should generate:

I NEED REST

If you look at the situation logically you will realise that for each input
subject there is an equivalent output subject, and that we have simply
chopped off the original subject and added the remainder of the sentence
to the appropriate new subject.

'I' is only a single character so we could check (IN$(1)) and, if this was
'I', PRINT 'YOU' would be added to the front of the remainder of the
input IN$(2 TO).

```
10 SCREEN
20    REPeat LOOP
30       AT #0, 1, 1 : IN$=GET$(1)
40       IN$=IN$ &" "
```

```
60          IF IN$(1)="I" THEN PRINT "YOU" &
            IN$(2 TO)
90          DUMMY$=INKEY$(500)
100         CLS #0
110     END REPeat LOOP
```

(Note that the SCREEN format and the GET$(1) routine are exactly the same as described for the last program.)

In the same way, the first three characters IN$(1 TO 3) could be checked against 'YOU' and replaced when necessary by 'I':

```
80          IF IN$(1 TO 3)="YOU" THEN PRINT "I"
            & IN$(4 TO)
```

If you try that out with a series of sentences you will see that it works OK until you type something like:

YOU ARE TIRED

which comes back as the rather unintelligent:

I ARE TIRED

We could get around this by checking for the phrases 'I AM' and 'YOU ARE' as well as 'I' and 'YOU' on their own, but notice that you must test for these first and add NEXT LOOP to the end of lines 50 and 70 to prevent a match also being found with 'I' and 'YOU' alone.

```
50          IF IN$(1 TO 4)="I AM" THEN PRINT
            "YOU ARE" & IN$(5 TO) : NEXT LOOP

70          IF IN$(1 TO 7)="YOU ARE" THEN PRINT
            "I AM" & IN$(8 TO) : NEXT LOOP
```

Wider dimensions

Although this method will work, the program soon gets very long-winded as a separate line is needed for each possibility as we must take into account the length of the matching word or phrase. Where many words are to be checked it is therefore better to use a multidimensional string array which can be compared with the input by a loop.

A convenient format is to have a two-dimensional array, I$(N,M), where the first dimension of each element, I$(N,0), is the input word or

phrase and the second dimension, I$(N,1), is the corresponding output
word or phrase. It is easier to avoid errors if these are entered into DATA
in matching pairs and READ in turn into the array. Start a new program
with these lines which SET_UP the array.

```
   20 SET_UP

11000 DEFine PROCedure SET_UP
11010   RESTORE
11030   DIM I$(3,1,7)
11100   DATA "I AM","YOU ARE","YOU ARE","I AM"
11110   DATA "I","YOU","YOU","I"
11200     FOR N=0 TO 3
11210       READ I$(N,0) : READ I$(N,1)
11220     END FOR N
11390 END DEFine SET_UP
```

We will use a looping sliding string search again, which for the moment
will just print out the corresponding word or phrase to that matched,
I$(N,1) (see **Flowchart 4.1**). One advantage of the sliding string search
here is that it will happily match embedded spaces in phrases as we have
not broken IN$ into 'words' before matching. (Note that the SCREEN
format and the GET$(1) routine are once again the same as described for
the last program.)

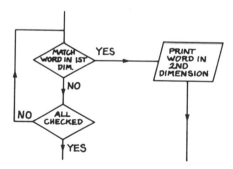

Flowchart 4.1:   **Using a Corresponding Reply.**

```
10 SCREEN
30   REPeat IN
40     AT #0, 1, 1 : IN$=GET$(1)
50       IN$=IN$&" "
60         FOR M=0 TO 3
```

```
70          IS%=I$(M,0) INSTR IN$
80            IF IS%>0 THEN EXIT M
90          END FOR M
120       DUMMY$=INKEY$(500)
130       CLS #0
140     END REPeat IN
```

The required response word is in the second dimension of the array (I$(M,1)) so we PRINT this when the loop is left.

```
100       PRINT I$(M,1)
```

To get a fuller reply we need to add back on the rest of the original sentence (see **Flowchart 4.2**). It is not difficult to define the 'rest of the sentence' as we must simply subtract the matched word from the front of the sentence. IS% points to the start of the matched word, and we can easily find the LENgth of this word as the word is stored in the first dimension of the array as I$(M,0). We therefore need to add IN$(IS%+LEN(I$(M,0)) on to the front of our response word. To make clear what is happening, the individual parts of the reply are printed separately in the upper window.

```
100       PRINT #2, I$(M,1),IN$(IS%+LEN(I$(M,0
          )) TO )
110       PRINT I$(M,1) & IN$(IS%+LEN(I$(M,0))
          TO )
```

Now when you try:

I AM CLEVER

the computer agrees:

YOU ARE CLEVER

Before you feel too clever try:

WE ARE STUPID

which may well surprise you when it gives the reply:

YOUD (!!!)

Flowchart 4.2:   A Fuller Reply.

If you think for a few moments you will see that one of our keywords is hiding inside another word in this particular sentence. If you cannot see it then try:

WE ARE INCOMPETENT

where the computer returns:

YOUNCOMPETENT

Although the keywords are tested for in turn, we EXIT the loop when a match is found so only the first match is reported. As the keyword is only checked for once in each sentence, embedded 'I' only causes problems when it precedes the keyword or there is no keyword in the sentence.

To get around this we must consider which keywords may cause problems. Although the letter 'I' is very common it is very rarely the last letter in a word, and so we could check that there is a space after the keyword. We must treat all keywords in the same way so add a space to

53

the end of them all. This can be done by changing the DATA. Note that there is no need to add spaces on to the end of the replies.

```
11100 DATA "I AM ","YOU ARE","YOU ARE ","I AM"
11110 DATA "I ","YOU","YOU ","I"
```

We now need to subtract one less character from IN$, as a space has been included as part of the keywords.

```
110     PRINT I$(M,1) & IN$(IS%+LEN(I$(M,0))
        -1 TO )
```

The computer will now readily agree on your incompetence.

   If the first key is not at the start of the sentence then everything before it will be ignored in the reply. For example the answer to:

WHAT IF I FALL?

will be:

YOU FALL?

Some strange results can still occur when two true keywords are present. For example:

WHAT IF YOU AND I FALL

gives

YOU FALL

and

WHAT IF I AND YOU FALL

replies

YOU AND YOU FALL

However adding more suitable keywords is easy and some combinations will just not be acceptable. To make the routine more general it is better to define the number of keywords as a variable, KW%, and use this in place of the actual number.

```
  60        FOR M=0 TO 3

11020    KW%=5
11030    DIM I$(KW%,1,7)
11120    DATA "WE ","WE","THEY ","THEY"
11200     FOR N=0 TO KW%
```

Now the answer to:

WHAT IF WE FALL?

is the more logical

WE FALL

Pointing to replies

So far our computer has displayed only slightly more intelligence than a parrot as it has merely regurgitated a slightly modified version of the input. The next stage, therefore, is to make it take some logical decisions on the basis of the input before it replies.

The numbers of subjects, SU%, verbs, VB%, and replies, RP%, are defined as variables so that the program can be easily expanded, and three arrays using these are set up. (As we have a zero element in the array these values are all one less than the number of words.) S$(n,n) is a two-dimensional array which is concerned with the subjects in the input and output sentences. The first dimension, (n,0) contains the recognised subject words and phrases allowed in the input, and the second dimension (n,1) contains the opposites which may be needed in the output. V$(n) holds the legal verbs, and R$(n) a series of corresponding replies.

```
  10 SCREEN
  20 SET_UP

11000 DEFine PROCedure SET_UP
11010   RESTORE
11020   SU%=26 : VB%=6 : RP%=6
11030   DIM S$(SU%,1,7) : DIM V$(VB%,7) :
        DIM R$(RP%,50)
```

The first six lines of DATA contain paired input and output subjects (see **Table 4.1**) and these are READ into corresponding dimensioned

Table 4.1: Pairs of Subjects in S$(n,n).

S$(n,0)	S$(n,1)
I HAVE	YOU HAVE
I'VE	YOU'VE
I AM	YOU ARE
I'M	YOU'RE
YOU HAVE	I HAVE
YOU'VE	I'VE
YOU ARE	I AM
YOU'RE	I'M
YOU	I
SHE HAS	SHE HAS
SHE IS	SHE IS
SHE'S	SHE'S
SHE	SHE
THEY'VE	THEY'VE
THEY ARE	THEY ARE
THEY'RE	THEY'RE
THEY	THEY
HE HAS	HE HAS
HE IS	HE IS
HE'S	HE'S
HE	HE
WE HAVE	WE HAVE
WE'VE	WE'VE
WE ARE	WE ARE
WE'RE	WE'RE
WE	WE
I	YOU

elements in the S$(n,n) array. As the pronouns ('I', 'YOU', etc) are frequently linked to other words to form phrases (such as 'I'VE') these combined forms are also included in the DATA. Notice that these are arranged in such an order that the most complete phrase containing a keyword is always found first. A space is added on to the end of each element, so that some clashing of partial matches is avoided and a space is automatically formed in the reply.

```
11040   DATA "I HAVE ","YOU HAVE ","I'VE ",
        "YOU'VE ","I AM ","YOU ARE ","I AM
        ","YOU'RE ","YOU HAVE ","I HAVE "
```

```
11050      DATA "YOU'VE ","I'VE ","YOU ARE ",
           "I AM ","YOU'RE ","I'M ","YOU ","I "
11060      DATA "SHE HAS ","SHE HAS ","SHE IS "
           ,"SHE IS","SHE'S","SHE'S","SHE","SHE"
11070      DATA "THEY'VE ","THEY'VE ","THEY ARE
           ","THEY ARE ","THEY'RE ","THEY'RE ",
           "THEY ","THEY "
11080      DATA "HE HAS ","HE HAS ","HE IS ","HE
           IS ","HE'S ","HE'S ","HE ","HE ","WE
           HAVE ","WE HAVE "
11090      DATA "WE'VE ","WE'VE ","WE ARE ","WE
           ARE ","WE'RE ","WE'RE ","WE ","WE ","I
           ","YOU "


11140      FOR N=0 TO SU%
11150        READ S$(N,0) : READ S$(N,1)
11160      END FOR N
```

The next DATA line contains the main verbs which are READ into VB%$(n). The verb 'to be' is omitted as its variations are so complicated, and many of its versions are already accounted for in the 'subject' check.

```
11100      DATA "HATE","LOVE","KILL","DISLIKE",
           "LIKE","FEEL","KNOW"


11170      FOR N=0 TO VB%
11180        READ V$(N)
11190      END FOR N
```

The last set of DATA contains the replies which are put into R$(n), before control returns to the main part of the program. To make things simple to understand and check at this stage, all the replies contain the original verb, although of course they could say anything.

```
11110    DATA "PROBABLY HATE YOU AS WELL","LOVE
         YOU TOO"
11120    DATA "KILL YOU","DISLIKE LOTS OF THINGS"
11130    DATA "LIKE CHIPS","FEEL POWERFUL?","KNOW
         EVERYTHING"
11200      FOR N=0 TO RP%
11210        READ R$(N)
11220      END FOR N
11230 END DEFine SET_UP
```

Matching

The input string is now compared with the list of subjects in the first dimension of S$(n,n) (see **Flowchart 4.3**). If there is no SUB_MATCH then the NEXT IN is requested, or else a subject match variable, SM%, is set to the element number at which a match was found. (The fact that no subject was found will be indicated by the fact that the input window (#0) does not clear before the next input.)

```
  30    REPeat IN
  40      AT #0, 1, 1 : IN$=GET$(1)
  50      IN$=IN$ & " "
  60      SUB_MATCH
  90      DUMMY$=INKEY$(500)
 100      CLS#0
 110    END REPeat IN

1000 DEFine PROCedure SUB_MATCH
1010    FOR M=0 TO SU%
1020      IS%=S$(M,0) INSTR IN$
1030        IF IS%>0 THEN
1050          SM%=M
1060          RETurn
1070        END IF
1090    END FOR M
1100      NEXT IN
1110 END DEFine SUB_MATCH
```

The verb array is now compared with IN$. If no verb is found then the input is rejected, or else the VERB_MATCH variable, VM%, is set.

```
  70     VERB_MATCH

2000 DEFine PROCedure VERB_MATCH
2010    FOR M=0 TO VB%
2020      IS%=V$(M) INSTR IN$
2030        IF IS%>0 THEN
2040          VM%=M
2060          RETurn
2070        END IF
2080    END FOR M
2090      NEXT IN
2100 END DEFine VERB_MATCH
```

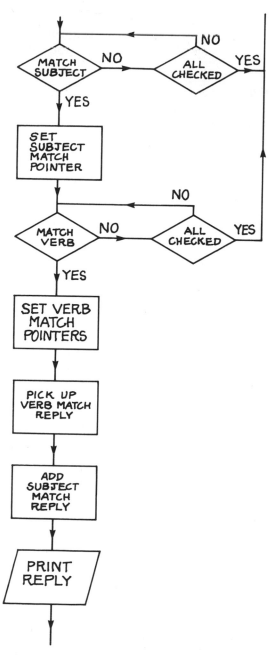

Flowchart 4.3:   Setting Match Pointers.

Making reply
Now that the subject and verb have been identified, we can pick up the appropriate reply by using VM% as a pointer to the reply array, R$(n).

```
 80      REPLY

3000 DEFine PROCedure REPLY
3010   RL$=R$(VM%)
```

In the simplest case we can just add the appropriate subject to the front of RL$ before we print it.

```
3060   RL$=S$(SM%,0) & RL$
3150   PRINT RL$
3190 END DEFine REPLY
```

Now, for example, if you type in:

I HATE COMPUTERS

the program will reply with

I PROBABLY HATE YOU AS WELL

and:

I KNOW A LOT

generates:

I KNOW EVERYTHING

Alternative subjects
If you prefer the machine to agree with you rather than trying to beat you at your own game, then just change the subject added to RL$ to the second element of the array (the 'opposite').

```
3060   RL$=S$(SM%,1) & RL$
```

Now:

I KNOW A LOT

generates:

YOU KNOW EVERYTHING

For more variety you can pick the subject at random from the first or
second element, so that the reply is not predictable.

```
3060    RL$=S$(SM%,RND(1)) & RL$
```

Putting the subject in context

It would be more sensible altogether if we chose the correct subject
according to the context of the reply, but to do that we must have markers
in the reply array. We will use a slash sign, '/', to indicate that the word in
the first dimension of the subject array is to be used, and an asterisk '*' to
indicate that the word in the second dimension is to be used.

```
11110    DATA "/PROBABLY HATE YOU AS WELL",
         "/LOVE YOU TOO"
11120    DATA "/KILL YOU","*DISLIKE LOTS OF
         THINGS"
11130    DATA "/LIKE CHIPS","*FEEL POWERFUL"
         ,"*KNOW EVERYTHING"
```

We can search the reply string, R$(VM%), pointed to by the verb
marker, VM%, for a slash sign, '/'. If a slash sign is found then the
contents of the first dimension of the subject array, S$(SM%,0), are
added to the reply, RL$, less the first character (the slash sign, see
Flowchart 4.4).

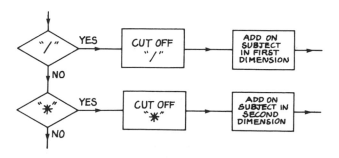

Flowchart 4.4:   Putting the Subject in Context.

```
3000 DEFine PROCedure REPLY
3010    RL$=R$(VM%)
3030    PRINT #2, RL$
3040    IS%="/" INSTR RL$
3050     IF IS%>0 THEN
3060       RL$=S$(SM%,0) & RL$(IS%+1 TO )
3080     END IF
```

If no slash sign is found in the reply, a second search is made for an asterisk, '*'. If this is found then the second dimension of S$(n,n) is used in the same way.

```
3090    IS%="*" INSTR RL$
3100     IF IS%>0 THEN
3110       RL$=S$(SM%,1) & RL$(IS%+1 TO )
3130     END IF
3150    PRINT RL$
3190 END DEFine REPLY
```

Now:

I LOVE ME

will give:

I LOVE YOU TOO

but:

I FEEL POWERFUL

produces:

YOU FEEL POWERFUL

Inserting into sentences

To make things simple we have always started our reply sentences with the subject, but in real life this is not always the case. Now that we have markers in the replies to indicate what type of subject is to be added, we can also use them to indicate where in the reply to insert this word or phrase. First we will amend the DATA so that the word to be inserted is never at the start, to make the insertion process obvious.

```
11110    DATA "DO YOU REALISE THAT /PROBABLY
         HATE YOU AS WELL","WELL /LOVE YOU TOO"
11120    DATA "IF /DON'T KILL YOU FIRST","SO
         WHAT /DISLIKE LOTS OF THINGS ESPECIALLY
         * "
11130    DATA "DO /LIKE CHIPS","WHY DO *FEEL
         POWERFUL?","*THINK *KNOW EVERYTHING"
```

(Note that the space after the asterisk in the DISLIKE reply is essential as a marker must not be the last character in a reply string.)

We actually already have a record of where to insert the word as IS% tells us where in the reply the slash or asterisk was found. All we need to do is to take the part of the reply before the marker (RL$(1 TO IS%−1)), add the correct version of S$(SM%,n), and then the rest of the reply (RL$(IS%+1 TO)).

```
3060        RL$=RL$(1 TO IS%-1) & S$(SM%,0)
            & RL$(IS%+1 TO )

3110        RL$=RL$(1 TO IS%-1) & S$(SM%,1)
            & RL$(IS%+1 TO )
```

Now:

I WILL KILL HIM

produces:

IF I DON'T KILL YOU FIRST

and:

I DISLIKE COMPUTERS

gives:

SO WHAT YOU DISLIKE LOTS OF THINGS

Although we are now inserting the subject into the reply sentence more naturally, we are only dealing with one subject per sentence. Some more minor modifications will allow us to insert any number of subjects into a sentence.

63

```
11120    DATA "IF /DON'T KILL YOU FIRST","SO
         WHAT /DISLIKE LOTS OF THINGS ESPECIALLY
          * "
11130    DATA "DO /LIKE CHIPS","WHY DO *FEEL
         POWERFUL?","*THINK *KNOW EVERYTHING"
```

We need to define the initial reply (RL$) as R$(VM%) and then REPeat
the CHECK for markers until no more are found (IS% = 0) when we
EXIT the CHECK loop (**Flowchart 4.5**).

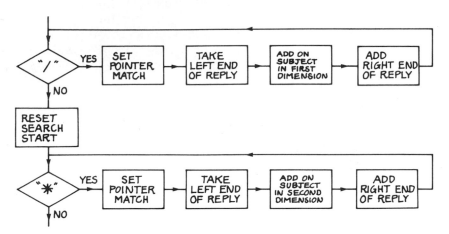

Flowchart 4.5:   Inserting into a Sentence.

```
3000 DEFine PROCedure REPLY
3010    RL$=R$(VM%)
3020      REPeat CHECK
3030        PRINT #2,RL$
3040        IS%="/" INSTR RL$
3050          IF IS%>0 THEN
3060             RL$=RL$(1 TO IS%-1) & S$(SM%,0)
                 & RL$(IS%+1 TO )
3070      NEXT CHECK
3080          END IF
3090        IS%="*" INSTR RL$
3100          IF IS%>0 THEN
3110             RL$=RL$(1 TO IS%-1) & S$(SM%,1)
                 &  RL$(IS%+1 TO )
3120      NEXT CHECK
3130          END IF
```

```
3140          IF IS%=0 THEN
3150             PRINT RL$
3160      EXIT CHECK
3170          END IF
3180      END REPeat CHECK
3190 END DEFine REPLY
```

Now:

I KNOW EVERYTHING

produces:

YOU THINK YOU KNOW EVERYTHING

and:

I DISLIKE COMPUTERS

gives

SO WHAT I DISLIKE LOTS OF THINGS ESPECIALLY YOU

OBJECTions on the SUBJECT

Everything is starting to look rosy until you try something like:

I HATE YOU

which replies

DO YOU REALISE THAT YOU PROBABLY HATE YOU AS WELL

The problem here is that we are jumping out of the search routine as soon as the first match is found, and that although we are checking for the subject 'I' we are finding the object 'YOU' first. As 'YOU' comes before 'I' in the subject array this is found first, in spite of the fact that it comes later in the sentence.

As we cannot practically mimic all the intricacies of the human brain we will have to make the assumption that the subject always comes before the verb, and the object after it. In the program so far we have been checking for the subject before we checked for the verb, so we will have to reverse that order.

```
60      VERB_MATCH
70      SUB_MATCH
```

The verb position in the input is the value of IS% when a verb is found, so we will save that as a verb position, VP%, pointer.

```
2000 DEFine PROCedure VERB_MATCH
2010   FOR M=0 TO VB%
2020     IS%=V$(M) INSTR IN$
2030       IF IS%>0 THEN
2040          VM%=M
2050          VP%=IS%
2060            RETurn
2070        END IF
2080    END FOR M
2090 END DEFine VERB_MATCH
```

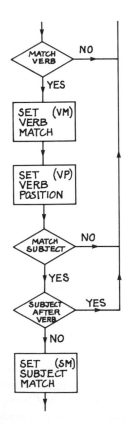

Flowchart 4.6:   Rejecting Object Matches.

Now when a match with the subject array is found we can compare that position, IS%, with the stored verb pointer, VP%, and reject the match if the match is positioned after the verb (see **Flowchart 4.6**).

```
1000 DEFine PROCedure SUB_MATCH
1010    FOR M=0 TO SU%
1020       IS%=S$(M,0) INSTR IN$
1030          IF IS%>0 THEN
1040             IF IS% < VP% THEN
1050                SM%=M
1060                   RETurn
1070             END IF
1080          END IF
1090    END FOR M
1100    NEXT IN
1110 END DEFine SUB_MATCH
```

A change of tense

Although both 'LIKE' and 'DISLIKE' contain the sequence 'L-I-K-E', we find 'DISLIKE' correctly as it is before 'LIKE' in the array. But if we change to the past tense of the verb it may or may not be found. With the first five verbs the situation is straightforward as to change to the past tense we just add on a 'D' at the end of the present tense. Both forms are therefore accepted.

HATE	HATED
LOVE	LOVED
KILL	KILLED
DISLIKE	DISLIKED
LIKE	LIKED

However, with the last two verbs the word changes completely, so there can be no simple match. Although we might get away with checking for 'KN', as this is a rare combination, there is no practical way we can use such a common group as 'FE' as a keyword.

FEEL	FELT
KNOW	KNEW

It is easier if we treat all verbs in the same way and, if there are no constraints on memory, then we can simply put all the possible versions into the verb array in pairs.

```
11020    SU%=26 : VB%=13 : RP%=6
11100    DATA "HATE","HATED","LOVE","LOVED",
         "KILL","KILLED","DISLIKE","DISLIKED"
11105    DATA "LIKE","LIKED","FEEL","FELT",
         "KNOW","KNEW"
```

Unless we want to have different replies for the different tenses, we will now have to divide the verb match variable, VM%, by two, to point to the correct reply for both forms.

```
2040        VM%=INT(M/2)
```

CHAPTER 5
Expert Systems

A human expert is someone who knows a great deal about a particular subject and who can give you sensible advice ('expert opinion') on it. Such expertise is only acquired after long training and a great deal of experience, so unfortunately real experts are few and far between. In addition they are often not on hand when a problem needs to be solved.

Scientists have therefore applied themselves to the problem of producing computer programs which mimic the functions of such human experts. Such programs have the advantage that they can be copied very easily to produce an infinite number of experts, and of course they do not need tea-breaks, sleep, pay-rises, etc, either! Of course the computer must be totally logical and can still only follow pre-programmed instructions entered by the programmer. It is interesting to note that science fiction authors have envisaged problems when the ultimate experts (such as HAL in '2001: A Space Odyssey' or Isacc Asimov's positronic robots) are faced with alternative courses which conflict with more than one of their prime directives and produce not system crashes but 'pseudo-nervous breakdowns'.

Before we can start writing programs for expert systems we must ask ourselves how a human expert works.

Let us first consider the simplest situation where the expert's task is to find the answer to a known problem.

First of all he takes in information on the current task

Secondly he compares this with information stored in his brain and looks for a match

Finally he reports whether a match has been found or not

What we need here is simply a database program which tries to match the input against stored information (see **Flowchart 5.1**). A user-friendly system would accept natural language (see earlier) but to keep things simple here we will stick to a fixed input format. To start with, let's look at recognising animals by the sounds they make. We use a START PROCedure to set up two arrays: the question array, QU$(n), contains

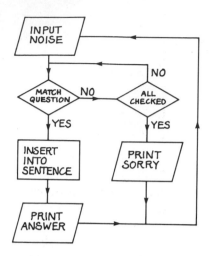

Flowchart 5.1: A Simple 'Expert'.

the sounds which are known, and each element of the answer array, AN$(n), contains the name of the relevant animal.

```
   10 SCREEN
   20 START

10000 DEFine PROCedure SCREEN
10010    MODE 4
10020    CLS #0 : CLS #1 : CLS #2
10030 END DEFine SCREEN

11000 DEFine PROCedure START
11010    RESTORE
11020    DIM QU$(4,5),AN$(4,5),IN$(5)
11030    DATA "MIAOW","CAT","WUFF","DOG","MOO"
         ,"COW","HOOT","OWL","NEIGH","HORSE"
11040      FOR N=0 TO 4
11050        READ QU$(N) : READ AN$(N)
11060      END FOR N
11070 END DEFine START
```

Now we just need to ask for a sound, using our GET$(1) FuNction, and compare it with the contents of QU$(n). If a match is found then an ANSWER PROCedure is called.

```
30    REPeat QUESTION
40      PRINT\"WHAT NOISE DOES IT MAKE? ";
50      IN$=GET$(1)
60        FOR N=0 TO 4
70          IF IN$=QU$(N) THEN ANSWER
80        END FOR N
90      PRINT"SORRY I DON'T KNOW THAT ONE"
100   END REPeat QUESTION

12000 DEFine PROCedure ANSWER
12010     PRINT"AN ANIMAL THAT ";QU$(N);"S IS
          A ";AN$(N)
12020   END REPeat QUESTION
12030 END DEFine ANSWER
```

Perhaps we should say at this point that our computer expert may well be better at this task than the human as it cannot make subjective judgements, become bored, or accidentally forget to check all of the information in its memory. On the other hand it is not very literate as it reports 'A OWL', etc. (We will leave you to tidy that up by adding a routine which checks whether the first letter of the answer array match is a vowel.)

Branching out

The example above is very simple as only one question is asked, and there is only one possible answer. In reality we need to be able to deal with more difficult problems, where the answer cannot be found without asking a whole series of questions. For example what should an expert do if he put the key in the ignition switch of his car and turned it, but nothing happened?

There could be a number of reasons for this:

FLAT BATTERY
BAD CONNECTIONS
SWITCH BROKEN
STARTER JAMMED
STARTER BROKEN
SOLENOID BROKEN

To find the cause he should follow a logical path and make a number of checks. The first thing to do is to check whether it is only the starter motor which is not working?

IS IGNITION LIGHT ON? (Y/N)

If the answer to this is 'N' then there is no power at the switch, so the cause must be one of the first three possibilities listed above. We can narrow things down more by finding out if the lights work:

DO LIGHTS WORK CORRECTLY? (Y/N)

If the answer is yes then the battery cannot be flat, and it must be connected to the light switch correctly, so presumably the switch is broken and a suggestion can be made that you replace it.

REPLACE IGNITION SWITCH

If the lights do not work then the connections should be checked.

ARE BATTERY CONNECTIONS OK? (Y/N)

If the answer is yes then the battery is flat so you must charge it (or push!).

CHARGE BATTERY OR PUSH CAR

In the same way a sequence of checks could be made to deal with the situation where there is power but the starter mechanism itself does not work (the last three possibilities). The simplest way to program this branching structure is a series of IF–THEN tests which call the appropriate PROCedures according to your response (see **Flowchart 5.2**).

```
   10 SCREEN
   20 START

10000 DEFine PROCedure SCREEN
10010    MODE 4
10020    CLS #0 : CLS #1 : CLS #2
10030 END DEFine SCREEN

11000 DEFine PROCedure START
11010    PRINT \"FAULT DIAGNOSIS"
11020    IGNITION
11030 END DEFine START

12000 DEFine PROCedure IGNITION
```

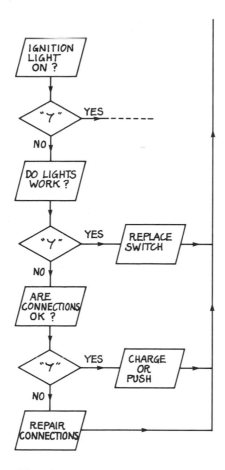

Flowchart 5.2:   A Branching 'Expert'.

```
12010    PRINT \"IS IGNITION LIGHT ON (Y/N) ";
12020    IN$=GET$(1)
12030      IF IN$="Y" THEN REST
12040      LIGHTS
12050 END DEFine IGNITION

13000 DEFine PROCedure LIGHTS
13010    PRINT \"DO LIGHTS WORK CORRECTLY (Y/N)";
13020    IN$=GET$(1)
13030      IF IN$="Y" THEN BATTERY
13040    PRINT \"REPLACE IGNITION SWITCH "
13050    START
13060 END DEFine LIGHTS
```

```
14000 DEFine PROCedure BATTERY
14010   PRINT \"ARE BATTERY CONNECTIONS OK
        (Y/N)";
14020   IN$=GET$(1)
14030     IF IN$="Y" THEN CHARGE
14040   PRINT \"REPAIR CONNECTIONS "
14050   START
14060 END DEFine BATTERY

15000 DEFine PROCedure CHARGE
15010   PRINT \"CHARGE BATTERY OR PUSH CAR "
15020   START
15030 END DEFine CHARGE

16000 DEFine PROCedure REST
16010   STOP
16020 END DEFine REST
```

This sort of program is relatively easy to write, but as usual is inefficient as it becomes longer and more complicated.

Pointing the way

A more efficient way to deal with the situation is to put the text into arrays and have pointers which direct you to the next question or reply, according to whether you answer yes or no to the current question (see **Flowchart 5.3**).

The format for entering the DATA for each branch point is then:

(TEXT), (pointer for 'YES'), (pointer for 'NO')

The first question was:

IS IGNITION LIGHT ON? (Y/N)   1

If the answer was 'N' then you need to ask the second question:

DO LIGHTS WORK CORRECTLY? (Y/N)   2

Otherwise you need to continue with the other part of the diagnosis (which we have not included but which would be point 7). We need to set up three arrays: OP$(n) contains the output (text), Y(n) the pointer for 'yes', and N(n) the pointer for 'no'. To make the program easy to modify

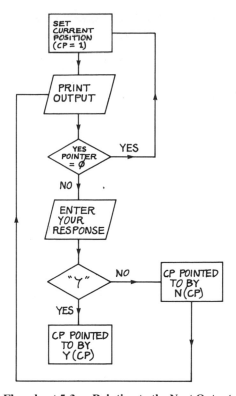

Flowchart 5.3:   Pointing to the Next Output.

a variable, NP%, is used for the number of points. The DATA is read in groups of three into each element in these arrays. Where the DATA point is a possible end of the program this is indicated by the Y(n) and N(n) pointers being set at zero. (Note that the SCREEN PROCedure is the same as in the last program, but that the rest of the program is new.)

```
   10 SCREEN
   20 START

11000 DEFine PROCedure START
11010    RESTORE
11020    NP%=7 : DIM OP$(NP%,30),Y(NP%),N(NP%)
11030    DATA "IS IGNITION LIGHT ON",7,2
11040    DATA "DO LIGHTS WORK CORRECTLY",3,4
11050    DATA "REPLACE SWITCH",0,0
11060    DATA "ARE BATTERY CONNECTIONS OK",5,6
11070    DATA "CHARGE BATTERY OR PUSH CAR",0,0
```

```
11080    DATA "REPAIR CONNECTIONS",0,0
11090    DATA "rest of program",0,0
11100     FOR M=1 TO NP%
11110       READ OP$(M) : READ Y(M) : READ N(M)
11120     END FOR M
11130 END DEFine START
```

The actual running routine is very simple. A pointer, CP%, is used to indicate the current position in the array: to begin with this is set to 1, and the first text pointed. If this is an end point, Y(CP%) = 0, (hardly likely just yet!) then we EXIT QUESTION and CP% is reset to 1 when the sequence is RESTARTed. If a real pointer is present then the REPeat QUESTION loop requests an INPUT. If the input is 'Y' then CP% is set to the value contained in the appropriate element of the Y(n) array, otherwise it is set to the value contained in the N(n) array.

```
30    REPeat RESTART
40        UNDER 1 : PRINT \\"FAULT DIAGNOSIS"
          : UNDER 0
50        CP%=1
60          REPeat QUESTION
70            PRINT \OP$(CP%);" ";
80              IF Y(CP%)=0 THEN EXIT QUESTION
90            IN$=GET$(1)
100             IF IN$="Y" THEN CP%=Y(CP%) :
                NEXT QUESTION
110           CP%=N(CP%)
120         END REPeat QUESTION
130   END REPeat RESTART
```

A parallel approach

An alternative to the sequential branching method described above is the parallel approach which always asks all the possible questions before it reaches its conclusion. This method usually takes longer than following an efficient tree structure but it is more likely to produce the correct answer as no points of comparison are omitted.

Let us consider how we might distinguish between various forms of transport.

We will consider eight features and mark 1 or 0 for the presence or absence of these in each of our five modes of transport (**Table 5.1**). If you look closely you will notice that the pattern of results varies for each of the different possibilities, so it must be possible to distinguish between them by thcsc features.

Table 5.1:   Presence or Absence of Features.

	bicycle	car	train	plane	horse
wheels	1	1	1	1	0
wings	0	0	0	1	0
engine	0	1	1	1	0
tyres	1	1	0	1	0
rails	0	0	1	0	0
windows	0	1	1	1	0
chain	1	0	0	0	0
steering	1	1	0	1	1

We will enter these values as DATA and then READ them into a two-dimensional array, FE(n,n), which will hold a copy of this pattern, together with a string array containing the names of the objects OB$(n). (Note that SCREEN is as before.)

```
  10 SCREEN
  20 START

11000 DEFine PROCedure START
11010   RESTORE
11020   DIM OB$(5,7),FE(5,8)
11030   DATA "BICYCLE",1,0,0,1,0,0,1,1
11040   DATA "CAR",1,0,1,1,0,1,0,1
11050   DATA "TRAIN",1,0,1,0,1,1,0,0
11060   DATA "PLANE",1,1,1,1,0,1,0,1
11070   DATA "HORSE",0,0,0,0,0,0,0,1
11080     FOR N=1 TO 5
11090       READ OB$(N)
11100         FOR M=1 TO 8
11110           READ FE(N,M)
11120         NEXT M
11130     NEXT N
11140 END DEFine START
```

We can now QUESTION whether the first feature is present or not, and then CHECK which modes of transport match at this particular point (see **Flowchart 5.4**).

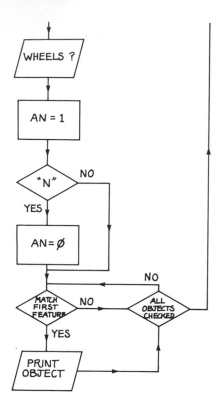

Flowchart 5.4:   A Parallel Approach.

```
  30    REPeat QUESTION
  50      PRINT \"DOES IT HAVE WHEELS "¡
          ¡ CHECK
 250    END REPeat QUESTION

12000 DEFine PROCedure CHECK
12010   IN$=GET$(1)
12020   AN%=1
12030     IF IN$="N" THEN AN%=0
12040       FOR N=1 TO 5
12050         IF FE(N,1)=AN% THEN PRINT OB$(N)
12060       END FOR N
12070 END DEFine CHECK
```

In this case, answering 'Y' will produce a printout of:

BICYCLE
CAR
TRAIN
PLANE

and answering 'N' will produce a printout of only:

HORSE

This clearly demonstrates a possible disadvantage of the parallel method as, although we have just shown that only a horse does not have wheels, the program insists that we still ask all the other questions before it commits itself. This is not really as silly as it seems at first, as if you answer 'Y' to the next question ('does it have wings') then you will see that the computer quite logically refuses to believe in flying horses.

We can now use the comparison CHECK PROCedure to test for all eight features in turn. We need to make slight modifications, adding an array pointer, AP%, which is incremented to check the next element of the feature array, FE(N,AP%), in each cycle (see **Flowchart 5.5**).

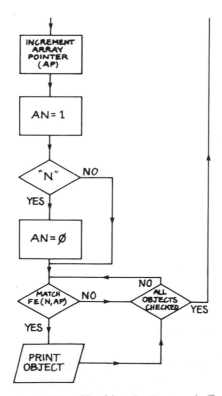

Flowchart 5.5:   Checking the Features in Turn.

```
 30     REPeat QUESTION
 50       PRINT \"DOES IT HAVE WHEELS "; :
          CHECK
 60       PRINT \"DOES IT HAVE WINGS "; :
          CHECK
 70       PRINT \"DOES IT HAVE AN ENGINE "; :
          CHECK
 80       PRINT \"DOES IT HAVE TYRES "; :
          CHECK
 90       PRINT \"DOES IT NEED RAILS "; :
          CHECK
100       PRINT \"DOES IT HAVE WINDOWS "; :
          CHECK
110       PRINT \"DOES IT HAVE A CHAIN "; :
          CHECK
120       PRINT \"IS IT STEERABLE "; :
          CHECK
130       AP%=0
250     END REPeat QUESTION

11020   DIM OB$(5,7),FE(5,8) : AP%=0

12020   AP%=AP%+1 : AN%=1

12050       IF FE(N,AP%)=AN% THEN PRINT OB$(N)
```

Top of the pops

The previous routine will print out a list of matches for each individual
question as it proceeds, but it does not actually tell us which set of DATA
is an overall match for the answers to all the questions. We can produce a
SCORE which shows how well the answers match the DATA by having a
success array element, SU(n), for each object, which is only incremented
when a match is found, FE(N,AP%) = AN% (see **Flowchart 5.6**).

```
200     PRINT \"SCORE"
210       FOR N=1 TO 5
220         PRINT OB$(N),SU(N)
230           SU(N)=0
240       END FOR N

11020   DIM OB$(5,7),FE(5,8) : AP%=0 : DIM SU(5)
12050       IF FE(N,AP%)=AN% THEN PRINT OB$(N)
            : SU(N)=SU(N)+1
```

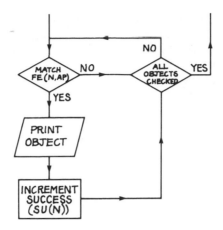

Flowchart 5.6:   Measuring Success.

If a complete match is found then SU(n) will be equal to 8. Where one or more points was incorrect, the score will be lowered, but scoring in this way is particularly useful where the correct answers to the questions are more a matter of opinion than fact (eg is a horse really steerable?), as the highest score actually obtained probably points to the correct answer anyway. (Notice that in this case each correct answer has equal weighting.)

Better in bits

You may have noticed that we just happened to use eight features for comparison and it may have occurred to you that this choice was not entirely accidental as there are eight bits in a byte. If we consider each feature as representing a binary digit (see **Table 5.2**), rather than an

Table 5.2:   Binary Weighted Features.

	bicycle	car	train	plane	horse
wheels	1	1	1	1	0
wings	0	0	0	2	0
engine	0	4	4	4	0
tyres	8	8	0	8	0
rails	0	0	16	0	0
windows	0	32	32	32	0
chain	64	0	0	0	0
steering	128	128	0	128	128
sum total	201	173	53	175	128

absolute value, then each object can be described by a single decimal number which is the sum of the binary digits, instead of eight separate values. We will convert to decimal with the least significant bit at the top so that starting from the top at 'wheels' each feature is equivalent to 1, 2, 4, 8, 16, 32, 64, 128 in decimal notation.

It is not too difficult to convert our 'score' of 1 to 8 into the appropriate binary value, as long as we remember that the decimal value of the binary digit, BV%, must double each time we move down and that we must only add the current binary value to the score if the answer was 'yes', AN% = 1 (see **Flowchart 5.7**).

If you consider for a moment, you will realise that we only need to keep track of the total number produced, SU%, by adding the binary values of the 'yes' answers — there is no need to loop through and check each part

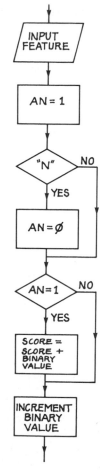

Flowchart 5.7:   Producing a Binary Score.

of the array contents each time, or even to have a two-dimensional array at all! The only DATA we need to enter are the overall decimal values for each object, DV(n), and when all the questions have been asked we can check these against the decimal value obtained by the binary conversion of the 'yes/no' answers, SU% (see **Flowchart 5.8**).

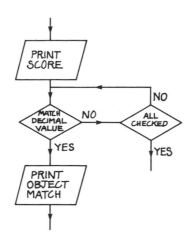

Flowchart 5.8:   Matching the Decimal Value.

```
40      BV%=1 : SU%=0

220        IF DV(N)=SU% THEN PRINT ,OB$(N) :
           NEXT QUESTION
230       END FOR N
240     REMark DELETED


11020     DIM OB$(5,7),DV(5)
11030     DATA "BICYCLE",201
11040     DATA "CAR",173
11050     DATA "TRAIN",53
11060     DATA "PLANE",175
11070     DATA "HORSE",128

11090        READ OB$(N)
11100        READ DV(N)
11110        REMark DELETED
11120        REMark DELETED

12040        IF AN%=1 THEN SU%=SU%+BV%
```

```
12050      BV%=BV%+BV%
12060      REMark DELETED
```

This approach obviously saves a lot of memory and time, as each array element takes up several bytes and must be located before it can be compared, so it is particularly useful where you are dealing with large amounts of information. But it does mean that you have to calculate the decimal equivalents of all of the bit patterns before you can use them, and it also gives you no clues when a complete match is not found. (Note that you cannot simply take the nearest decimal value here as the decimal equivalent value of each correct answer depends on its position.)

Of course you could do the calculations the hard way, but on the other hand you can easily DEFine a BIN FuNction to do the hard work for you. A row of eight dots is printed as a prompt and the required string of binary digits (N$) entered, and passed to BIN. This slices off each individual digit, starting from the least significant (righthand end). If the digit is 1 (note that SuperBASIC coercion allows direct comparison of string and simple variables) then the decimal value (DV%) is updated. When all eight digits have been checked, the final decimal value (DV%) is RETurned.

```
  1 CLS
  2 PRINT "........"
  3 INPUT N$
  4 PRINT BIN(N$)
  5 GO TO 2

30000 DEFine FuNction BIN(N$)
30010    DV%=0 : BD%=1
30020      FOR N=8 TO 1 STEP -1
30030        IF N$(N)=1 THEN DV%=DV%+BD%
30040        BD%=BD%+BD%
30050      END FOR N
30060    RETurn DV%
30070 END DEFine BIN
```

CHAPTER 6
Making your Expert System Learn for Itself

Although the expert systems described so far will function all right, they all require you to give them the correct rules on which to base their decisions in advance, which can be very tedious, or even downright impossible where the human expert is not really sure of the answer.

However it is also possible to construct an expert program which can learn from its mistakes and work out the decision rules for itself, which is, of course, what a human expert tends to do. The only requirement is that *you* have to tell it when (although not where) it goes wrong. This is obviously an advantage if you are not altogether sure of the correct rules yourself anyway. In this case we start out with a series of feature variables which we hope should enable us to distinguish between the different objects (outcomes) but without any predefined yes/no pattern of these features ('decision rule') to guide us. Instead we use the program itself to determine what the pattern should be.

We will work with our familiar transport example and start by setting up the variables. FE% is the number of features to be considered, 8, FE$(N) is an array containing the names of these features, FV(N) is an array which will hold the values which you give to each feature when you make input at any particular point (as 0 or 1), and RU(N) is an array which will hold the current overall values of the decision rule on each feature.

```
   10 SCREEN
   20 START

10000 DEFine PROCedure SCREEN
10010    MODE 4
10020    CLS #0 : CLS #1 : CLS #2
10030 END DEFine SCREEN

11000 DEFine PROCedure START
11010    RESTORE
11020    FE%=8 : DIM FE$(FE%,8),FV(FE%),RU(FE%)
```

```
11030      FOR N=1 TO FE%
11040        READ FE$(N)
11050      END FOR N
11060   DATA "WHEELS","WINGS","ENGINE","TYRES",
        "RAILS","WINDOWS","CHAIN","STEERING"
11070 END DEFine START
```

Each feature is considered in turn (see **Flowchart 6.1**) in the QUESTION PROCedure. First the current feature value, FV(N), for this cycle is set to 0, and then a 'yes/no' input IN$ is requested from the user on each point. If IN$ is 'Y', the feature value element, FV(N), is set to 1, but otherwise it remains set at 0. This will produce a pattern which describes the particular object (outcome) as a pattern of '0' and '1' in array FV(N).

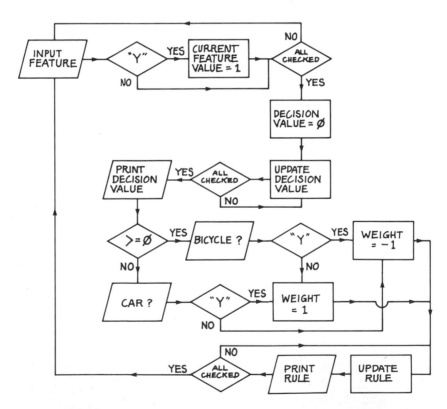

Flowchart 6.1:   Learning to Distinguish Between Two Objects.

```
50 REPeat QUESTION
60    FOR N=1 TO FE%
70      FV(N)=0
80      PRINT !FE$(N);
90      IN$=INKEY$(-1)
100     IN$=CHR$((CODE(IN$) || 32)-32)
110       IF IN$="Y" THEN FV(N)=1
120    END FOR N

200 END REPeat QUESTION
```

(Note that a simpler method of forcing upper case is used here, rather than the GET$ PROCedure, as only single character inputs are made which are easily modified.)

Now in UPDATE_DE the decision variable, DE%, is set to zero before being recalculated as the sum of the current value of DE% plus each of the feature values, FV(N), entered multiplied by the current decision rule values, RU(N).

```
130    UPDATE=DE

12000 DEFine PROCedure UPDATE_DE
12010   DE%=0
12020     FOR N=1 TO FE%
12030       DE%=((DE%*3)+(FV(N)*RU(N))*3))/3
12040     END FOR N
12050   PRINT \\"DE%= ";DE%
12060 END DEFine UPDATE_DE
```

Which is which?

To start with, we will consider the simplest situation where there are only two possibilities — a BICYCLE or a CAR. Initially we make the distinction between these quite arbitrarily by saying that if the final value of DE% is equal to or greater than 0 then it is a BICYCLE, whereas if DE% is less than 0 then it is a CAR. It does not really matter that this is not actually true as the system will soon correct itself. When the program has made a decision on the basis of the value of DE% it requests confirmation (or otherwise) of the result.

```
180    IF DE%>=0 THEN PRINT \"IS IT A BICYCLE
       "; : IN$=INKEY$(-1) : IN$=CHR$((CODE(
       IN$) || 32)-32) : PRINT IN$ : BICYCLE
```

```
190     IF DE%<0 THEN PRINT \"IS IT A CAR "; :
IN$=INKEY$(-1) : IN$=CHR$((CODE(IN$)
|| 32)-32) : PRINT IN$ : CAR
```

Three possible courses of action may be taken according to whether or not the computer's decision was confirmed by you.

If it was correct then effectively no action is taken as the weighting variable, WT%, is set to 0.

IF DE% was >=0, but the computer was wrong (and selected CAR), then the weighting variable, WT%, is set to −1.

If DE% was <0, but the computer was wrong (and selected BICYCLE), then WT% is set to +1.

```
13000 DEFine PROCedure BICYCLE
13010   IF IN$="Y" THEN WT%=0 : UPDATE_RULE
13020   WT%=-1 : UPDATE_RULE
13030 END DEFine BICYCLE

14000 DEFine PROCedure CAR
14010   IF IN$="Y" THEN WT%=0 : UPDATE_RULE
14020   WT%=1 : UPDATE_RULE
14030 END DEFine CAR
```

The effect of the weighting variable takes place in the UPDATE_RULE PROCedure in which we modify the values in the rule array, RU(N), pulling them down when they are too high, and pulling them up when they are too low.

```
15000 DEFine PROCedure UPDATE_RULE
15010   PRINT \"RULES"\
15020   FOR N=1 TO FE%
15030     RU(N)=((RU(N)*3)+(FV(N)*WT%)*3)/3
15040     PRINT RU(N),FE$(N)
15050   END FOR N
15060 END DEFine UPDATE_RULE
```

The way the system operates is best seen by a demonstration. Type RUN and then follow this sequence of entries. (Note that the punctuation has been designed to give a screen format which clearly indicates the relationship between your input values and the decision rule values.)

First of all enter these values:

WHEELS Y	WINGS N	ENGINE N	TYRES Y
RAILS N	WINDOWS N	CHAIN Y	STEERING Y

The program will return with a decision value, DE%, of 0, as this is the initial value and no modifications have yet taken place:

DE% = 0

As DE% is 0 then the system assumes that this is a BICYCLE and asks for confirmation, to which the answer is, of course, 'yes':

IS IT A BICYCLE? Y

The contents of the rule array, RU(N), are now printed out. This shows that the values have not changed from 0 as the correct answer was, by pure chance, obtained!

RULES

0	WHEELS
0	WINGS
0	ENGINE
0	TYRES
0	RAILS
0	WINDOWS
0	CHAIN
0	STEERING

Now try entering this sequence which describes a CAR:

WHEELS Y	WINGS N	ENGINE Y	TYRES Y
RAILS N	WINDOWS Y	CHAIN N	STEERING Y

DE% is still 0, so the wrong conclusion is reached and the wrong question is asked (BICYCLE) to which the answer must be 'no':

DE% = 0

IS IT A BICYCLE ? N

Now as a mistake was made the decision rule is modified by subtracting 1 from each value in the rule array where a 'yes' answer was given. The contents of the rule array are thus now:

RULES

−1	WHEELS
0	WINGS
−1	ENGINE
−1	TYRES
0	RAILS
−1	WINDOWS
0	CHAIN
−1	STEERING

If you now enter the values which describe a CAR once more, the program will come up with the correct answer:

WHEELS Y	WINGS N	ENGINE Y	TYRES Y
RAILS N	WINDOWS Y	CHAIN N	STEERING Y

DE% = −5

IS IT A CAR ? Y

RULES

−1	WHEELS
0	WINGS
−1	ENGINE
−1	TYRES
0	RAILS
−1	WINDOWS
0	CHAIN
−1	STEERING

Before you feel too pleased with yourself, try giving it the values for a BICYCLE again, which it will get wrong!

WHEELS Y	WINGS N	ENGINE N	TYRES Y
RAILS N	WINDOWS N	CHAIN Y	STEERING Y

DE% = −3

IS IT A CAR ? N

RULES

0	WHEELS
0	WINGS
−1	ENGINE
0	TYRES
0	RAILS
−1	WINDOWS
1	CHAIN
0	STEERING

However the positive features which are common to the BICYCLE and the CAR are now automatically increased by 1, so that if you repeat this last sequence it will now produce the correct conclusion:

WHEELS Y	WINGS N	ENGINE N	TYRES Y
RAILS N	WINDOWS N	CHAIN Y	STEERING Y

DE% =1
IS IT A BICYCLE? Y

RULES

0	WHEELS
0	WINGS
−1	ENGINE
0	TYRES
0	RAILS
−1	WINDOWS
1	CHAIN
0	STEERING

The situation has now stabilised and the program will always recognise both CAR and BICYCLE correctly every time you enter the features which describe them:

WHEELS Y	WINGS N	ENGINE Y	TYRES Y
RAILS N	WINDOWS Y	CHAIN N	STEERING Y

DE% = −2

IS IT A CAR? Y

RULES

0	WHEELS
0	WINGS

−1	ENGINE
0	TYRES
0	RAILS
−1	WINDOWS
1	CHAIN
0	STEERING

Notice that the final value of DE% for a BICYCLE is 1, and for a CAR −2. If you look at the rule array values, you will see that these correspond in both number and position to the unique features which distinguish these objects (CHAIN for BICYCLE, and ENGINE and WINDOWS for CAR).

A wider spectrum

Although you have now managed to teach your computer something, it is not exactly earth-shattering to be able to distinguish between only two objects. Let's expand the system to deal with a wider spectrum of possibilities (see **Flowchart 6.2**).

To start with we need to define the number of objects (outcomes) we wish to be able to recognise, OB%, name them as DATA which we READ into a new array, OB$(OB%), change our decision rule array into a two-dimensional form, RU(FE%, OB%), which can hold rules for each of the objects separately, and set up a decision array, DE(N), to hold decision values for each object.

```
   20 START

11000 DEFine PROCedure START
11010    RESTORE
11020    FE%=8 : OB%=5 : DIM FE$(FE%,8),FV(FE%),
         RU(FE%,OB%),OB$(OB%,7),DE(OB%) : TS%=5
11030       FOR N=1 TO FE%
11040          READ FE$(N)
11050       END FOR N
11060    DATA "WHEELS","WINGS","ENGINE","TYRES",
         "RAILS","WINDOWS","CHAIN","STEERING"
11070       FOR N=1 TO OB%
11080          READ OB$(N)
11090       END FOR N
11100    DATA "BICYCLE","CAR","PLANE","TRAIN"
         ,"HORSE"
11110 END DEFine START
```

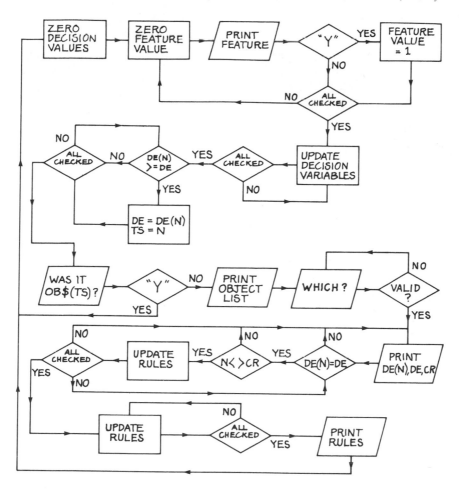

Flowchart 6.2:   Learning the Rules for a Wider Spectrum of Possibilities.

Rather than just having a single decision variable, DE%, we need here to determine a decision value for each object each time. In each cycle we must first set DE% to zero, and then zero every element in the decision array, DE(N), so that we start with a clean state for every object (ZERO_DE).

```
50      ZERO_DE

14000 DEFine PROCedure ZERO_DE
14010    DE%=0
14020      FOR N=1 TO OB%
```

```
14030          DE(N)=0
14040      END FOR N
14050 END DEFine ZERO_DE
```

Questions on the values for each feature are then entered in the same way as before.

```
40    REPeat QUESTION

60        FOR N=1 TO FE%
70          FV(N)=0
80          PRINT !FE$(N);
90          IN$=INKEY$(-1)
100         IN$=CHR$((CODE(IN$) || 32)-32)
110         PRINT !IN$;
120           IF IN$="Y" THEN FV(N)=1
130       END FOR N

200   END REPeat QUESTION
```

UPDATE_DV now updates each element of the decision array, DE(N), according to the status of the entered values, FV(N), and the contents of the appropriate rule array element, RU(N,M).

```
140      UPDATE_DV

15000 DEFine PROCedure UPDATE_DV
15010   FOR N=1 TO FE%
15020     FOR M=1 TO OB%
15030       DE(M)=((DE(M)*3)+((FV(N)*
              RU(N,M))*3))/3
15040     END FOR M
15050   END FOR N
15060 END DEFine UPDATE_DV
```

We now need to look to see if any of the DECISION values for any of the objects, DE(N), are greater than or equal to the overall decision value, DE%. If this is true then we set a 'top score', TS%, variable equal to the number of the object producing the best match, N.

```
150     DECISION

16000 DEFine PROCedure DECISION
16010   FOR N=1 TO OB%
16020     IF DE(N)>=DE% THEN DE%=DE(N) : TS%=N
16030   END FOR N
16040 END DEFine DECISION
```

The best guess of the system is that this is the correct answer, so once again it asks for confirmation, and simply returns for a new input without making any changes if the answer was correct.

```
160     ANSWER

17000 DEFine PROCedure ANSWER
17010   PRINT \"WAS IT ";OB$(TS%);" ";
17020   IN$=INKEY$(-1)
17030   IN$=CHR$((CODE(IN$) || 32) -32)
17040   PRINT IN$
17050   IF IN$="Y" THEN NEXT QUESTION
17060 END DEFine ANSWER
```

However, if the answer needs correction, the names and numbers of all of the objects are printed out and you are asked for the number of the correct answer, CR%. (The limitations on CR% prevent you crashing the program by entering an illegal value.)

```
170     CORRECTION

18000 DEFine PROCedure CORRECTION
18010   FOR N=1 TO OB%
18020     PRINT \N,OB$(N);
18030   END FOR N
18040   PRINT \\"WHICH WAS IT? ";
18050   IN$=INKEY$(-1)
18060   CR%=CODE(IN$)-48 : IF CR%<1 OR CR%>5
          THEN CORRECTION
18070   PRINT CR%
18080 END DEFine CORRECTION
```

To UPDATE_RULES we must first make a check to determine whether the decision value for each object, DE(N), is greater than or equal to the overall decision value, DE%, AND whether the object being considered is NOT the correct answer. If *both* of these are true then the rules are updated again by subtracting the correct feature values, FV(N), to bias in favour of the correct answer.

```
180      UPDATE_RULES

19000 DEFine PROCedure UPDATE_RULES
19010     FOR N=1 TO OB%
19020      IF DE(N)>=DE% AND N<>CR% THEN
19030        FOR M=1 TO FE%
19040          RU(M,N)=((RU(M,N)*3)-
                 (FV(M)*3))/3
19050        END FOR M
19060     ELSE NEXT N
19070       END IF
19080     END FOR N
```

Then the correct feature values, FV(N), are added to the rule array for the correct object to bias in the opposite direction.

```
19090     FOR M=1 TO FE%
19100       RU(M,CR%)=((RU(M,CR%)*3)+
               (FV(M)*3))/3
19110     NEXT M
19120 END DEFine UPDATE_RULES
```

Finally DISPLAY_RULES prints out the status of the rule arrays so that you can see what is happening.

```
190      DISPLAY_RULES

20000 DEFine PROCedure DISPLAY_RULES
20010   CLS #2 : CLS #3
20020   FOR M=1 TO OB%
20030     AT #2,3,M-1 : PRINT #2,DE(M);"
          ";DE%;"        ";CR%
20040      FOR N=1 TO FE%
20050        AT #3,(N*3)-3,M-1 : PRINT
             #3,RU(N,M);
20060      END FOR N
```

```
20070    END FOR M
20080    PRINT
20090 END DEFine DISPLAY_RULES
```

To make the whole program easier to understand we will use the capabilities of the QL to produce a comprehensive screen status format (see **Figure 6.1**) with multiple windows. These are produced by the SCREEN_SET PROCedure and then LABELled appropriately. Although we will omit any discussion on the details of this 'decorative' aspect of the program, we should explain that the main action takes place in the default window (right half of screen), with printouts of DE(N), DE% and CE% in window #2, the rules in window #3, and various labels in windows #4, #5 and #6.

Note that a separate SCREEN PROCedure is defined which not only clears the whole screen to start with but also provides you with a safety net which can easily return you to an acceptable format for listing the program. The two parameters passed to SCREEN are PAPER and INK, respectively, hence typing SCREEN 6,0 as a direct command before LIST will automatically return the full screen area and produce a black listing on a white background.

```
   10 SCREEN 0,6 : SCREEN_SET
   30 LABEL

10000 DEFine PROCedure SCREEN_SET
10010    MODE 0
10020    CLS #0
10030      INK #0,7
10100    WINDOW #1,230,200,257,16
10110      BORDER #1,3,6
10120      CSIZE #1,2,0
10130      PAPER #1,5
10140      INK #1,0
10150      CLS #1
10200    WINDOW #2,140,50,105,32
10220      CSIZE #2,0,0
10240      INK #2,2
10250      CLS #2
10300    OPEN #3,SCR_170X60A85X100
10310      BORDER #3,3,2
10320      CSIZE #3,0,0
10330      PAPER #3,6
10340      INK #3,0
```

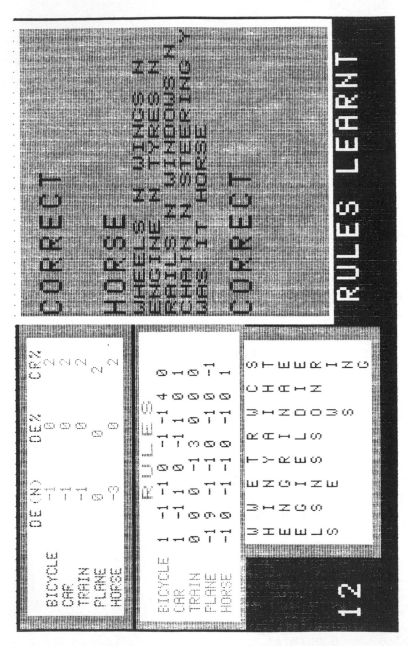

Figure 6.1:   A Learning Expert.

```
10350      CLS #3
10400    OPEN#4,SCR_175X90A80X155
10410      BORDER #4,5,2
10420      CSIZE #4,0,0
10430      INK #4,1,0
10440      PAPER #4,6
10450      CLS #4
10500    OPEN#5,SCR_230X70A26X90
10510      BORDER #5,3,2
10520      CSIZE #5,0,0
10530      INK #5,4
10540      PAPER #5,6
10550      CLS #5
10600    OPEN #6,SCR_230X70A26X18
10610      BORDER #6,5,2
10620      CSIZE #6,0,0
10630      INK #6,1,4
10640      PAPER #6,6
10650      CLS #6
10700 END DEFine SCREEN_SET

20000 DEFine PROCedure SCREEN (A,B)
20010    WINDOW #2,460,200,26,16
20020    PAPER #2,A
20030    INK #2,B
20040    CLS #2
20050 END DEFine SCREEN

13000 DEFine PROCedure LABEL
13010    AT #6,11,0 : CSIZE #6,1,0 : PRINT
         #6,"DE(N)   DE%   CR%" : CSIZE #6,0,0
13020      FOR N=1 TO OB%
13030        AT #6,1,N : PRINT #6,OB$(N)
13040        AT #5,1,N : PRINT #5,OB$(N)
13050      END FOR N
13060      FOR N=1 TO FE%
13070        FOR M=1 TO 8
13080          AT #4,(N*3)-2,M-1
13090          PRINT #4,FE$(N,M)
13100          AT #5,15,0 : CSIZE #5,3,0 : PRINT
               #5,"RULES" : CSIZE #5,0,0
13110        END FOR M
13120      END FOR N
13130 END DEFine LABEL
```

Once again a demonstration is the best way to understand what is happening so enter the following sequence:

WHEELS Y   WINGS N
ENGINE N   TYRES Y
RAILS N   WINDOWS N
CHAIN Y   STEERING Y

The program will come back with the erroneous conclusion that it was a HORSE, so you must tell it that this was wrong, when it will ask you for the correct answer (BICYCLE = 1):

WAS IT HORSE N

1	BICYCLE
2	CAR
3	TRAIN
4	PLANE
5	HORSE

WHICH WAS IT 1

The status of the various decision and rule arrays are now printed out for your information, in the windows on the lefthand side of the screen.

	DE (N)	DE%	CR%
BICYCLE	0	0	1
CAR	0	0	1
TRAIN	0	0	1
PLANE	0	0	1
HORSE	0	0	1

RULES

BICYCLE	1	0	0	1	0	0	1	1
CAR	−1	0	0	−1	0	0	−1	−1
TRAIN	−1	0	0	−1	0	0	−1	−1
PLANE	−1	0	0	−1	0	0	−1	−1
HORSE	−1	0	0	−1	0	0	−1	−1

```
W    W    E    T    R    W    C    S
H    I    N    Y    A    I    H    T
E    N    G    R    I    N    A    E
E    G    I    E    L    D    I    E
L    S    N    S    S    O    N    R
S         E              W         I
                        S         N
                                  G
```

If you look closely you will see that the features which have caused alterations in the rule arrays are wheels, tyres, chain and steering — which are all features which we defined as part of a BICYCLE but which are not found in a HORSE. In addition you will see that the values for these features in the BICYCLE rule array are now all +1, whilst the values for these features for all the other objects are all now −1. Now give it the features of a CAR, which it thinks is a BICYCLE, and then correct it. Notice that the rule arrays for BICYCLE and CAR are now amended to take into account the new information.

WHEELS Y   WINGS N
ENGINE Y   TYRES Y
RAILS N   WINDOWS Y
CHAIN N   STEERING Y

WAS IT BICYCLE N

1	BICYCLE
2	CAR
3	TRAIN
4	PLANE
5	HORSE

WHICH WAS IT 2

	DE (N)	DE%	CR%
BICYCLE	3	3	2
CAR	−3	3	2
TRAIN	−3	3	2
PLANE	−3	3	2
HORSE	−3	3	2

RULES

	WHEELS	WINGS	ENGINE	TYRES	RAILS	WINDOWS	CHAIN	STEERING
BICYCLE	0	0	−1	0	0	−1	1	0
CAR	0	0	1	0	0	1	−1	0
TRAIN	−1	0	0	−1	0	0	−1	−1
PLANE	−1	0	0	−1	0	0	−1	−1
HORSE	−1	0	0	−1	0	0	−1	−1

Next give it a PLANE, which it decides is a CAR, and correct it again.

WHEELS Y   WINGS Y
ENGINE Y   TYRES Y
RAILS N   WINDOWS Y
CHAIN N   STEERING Y

WAS IT CAR N

1	BICYCLE
2	CAR
3	TRAIN
4	PLANE
5	HORSE

WHICH WAS IT 4

And now a TRAIN, which it still gets wrong!

WHEELS Y   WINGS N
ENGINE Y   TYRES N
RAILS N   WINDOWS Y
CHAIN N   STEERING N

WAS IT PLANE N

1	BICYCLE
2	CAR
3	TRAIN

4	PLANE
5	HORSE

WHICH WAS IT 3

And finally a HORSE, which comes out as a PLANE!

WHEELS N	WINGS N
ENGINE N	TYRES N
RAILS N	WINDOWS N
CHAIN N	STEERING Y

WAS IT PLANE N

1	BICYCLE
2	CAR
3	TRAIN
4	PLANE
5	HORSE

WHICH WAS IT 5

If you continue to feed your expert information then eventually it will get the right answer every time. How long this will take depends upon the extent of the differences between the features of the objects, and on the order in which the objects are presented to the expert. Be warned that it can take a long time before it becomes infallible! Here is one sequence which eventually was right every time.

PLANE (TRAIN)	CAR (PLANE)	BICYCLE (YES)
CAR (YES)	PLANE (CAR)	PLANE (YES)
HORSE (YES)	PLANE (BICYCLE)	CAR (PLANE)
PLANE (CAR)	PLANE (CAR)	CAR (PLANE)
CAR (YES)	PLANE (CAR)	PLANE (YES)
CAR (YES)	PLANE (YES)	HORSE (YES)
BICYCLE (YES)	TRAIN (CAR)	TRAIN (YES)
BICYCLE (YES)	CAR (PLANE)	CAR (YES)
PLANE (CAR)	PLANE (YES)	CAR (PLANE)
CAR (YES)	PLANE (YES)	CAR (YES)
BICYCLE (CAR)	CAR (YES)	PLANE (YES)
TRAIN (YES)	HORSE (YES)	BICYCLE (YES)

As the final scale of values ranged from +6 to −2 you should not be surprised that it took a long time to get there.

RULES

	WHEELS	WINGS	ENGINE	TYRES	RAILS	WINDOWS	CHAIN	STEERING
BICYCLE	1	0	−1	1	0	−2	3	0
CAR	−1	4	1	0	−1	1	−2	0
TRAIN	0	−1	1	−2	2	1	−1	−2
PLANE	−2	6	0	0	−1	0	−2	−2
HORSE	−1	0	0	−1	0	0	−1	0

Automatic digestion of the data

Although our expert now manages to sort out the rules for itself, we are still left with the tedious job of holding a 'conversation' with it, whilst it builds up the correct pattern in its rule arrays. In a real application of such an expert system it would be much better if we could feed it a mass of collected information on a subject area and the conclusions, and then leave it alone to digest this and come up with the rules automatically in its own good time.

In fact it is not too difficult to modify our existing program to produce an 'automatic' mode which crunches information provided as DATA.

First of all we need to enter that information in a fixed format containing the name of the particular object and 'Y' and 'N' answers for each feature, in the correct order.

```
25000 REMark INFORMATION STORE
25010   DATA "BICYCLE","Y","N","N","Y",
        "N","N","Y","Y"
25020   DATA "CAR","Y","N","Y","Y",
        "N","Y","N","Y"
25030   DATA "TRAIN","Y","N","Y","N",
        "Y","Y","N","N"
25040   DATA "PLANE","Y","Y","Y","Y",
        "N","Y","N","Y"
25050   DATA "HORSE","N","N","N","N",
        "N","N","N","Y"
25060   DATA "END"
```

We now introduce a READER PROCedure, called at the start of the QUESTION loop, which, for the moment, just READs and PRINTs out the name (N$) of the object currently being examined.

```
45 READER

26000 DEFine PROCedure READER
26030    READ N$
26100    CSIZE 3,1 : PRINT N$ : CSIZE 2,0
26110 END DEFine READER
```

The 'Y' and 'N' answers for each feature are also READ in turn, as IN$, in a replacement for the previous INKEY$ check in the QUESTION loop.

```
90 READ IN$
```

In the ANSWER PROCedure, we need to compare the name of the object being examined (N$) with the name of the top-scoring object (OB$(TS%)) selected by our expert. If a match is found then 'CORRECT' is printed.

```
14020 IF OB$(TS%)=N$ THEN
14030    CSIZE 3,1 : PRINT \"CORRECT"\\ :
         CSIZE 2,0
14040    NEXT QUESTION
14050 END IF
```

In the CORRECTION PROCedure we need to compare the name of the item currently being examined (N$) with the names of each of the objects (OB$(N)) which are known by our expert. The best way to do this is to insert a check inside the listing loop which sets CR% to N when there is a match. The original INKEY$ and following validation check must also be removed.

```
17025 IF OB$(N)=N$ THEN CR%=N
17050 REMark DELETED
17060 REMark DELETED
```

Once those changes have been made you can sit back, or perhaps indulge in a cup of coffee, as you watch your expert hard at work!

Round and round

As it stands the program will end when all of the objects have been examined once which, as you should have already noticed, is not enough to build the correct rules. We can force repeat cycling by checking whether the 'END' message following the real DATA has been detected, and RESTOREing to the appropriate line number. Notice that we must READ N$ again after the RESTORE.

```
26040      IF N$="END" THEN
26050          RESTORE 27000
26080          READ N$
26090      END IF
```

To be able to see how well our expert is doing and to be able to congratulate him when he has finished his task, we need to keep track of how many cycles of testing have been completed, and whether full success has been achieved. Two new variables are defined. CY% is the number of cycles of comparisons completed, and SU% is the success achieved. SU% must be incremented in the ANSWER PROCedure, reset on RESTORE, and be compared with the number of objects to be correctly identified (5). A printout of the current cycle is produced in the bottom left hand corner of the screen on channel #0, so that you can assess progress, and a 'RULES LEARNT' message appears when SU% reaches 5.

```
  5 CY%=1 : SU%=0

14040     SU%=SU%+1 : NEXT QUESTION

26010      IF SU%=5 THEN STOP
26020     AT #0,0,0 : CSIZE #0,3,1 : PRINT #0,
          CY% : CSIZE #0,0,0

26070         SU%=0
```

When you test out this automated version you will discover *six* cycles of the DATA are required to guarantee successful recognition of the five modes of transport as the DATA is entered. However, if you switch the positions of the BICYCLE and the HORSE this reduces to only *four* cycles. With PLANE swapped with BICYCLE only four cycles are again needed, but with BICYCLE and CAR switched the requirement rises to no less than *twelve* cycles! It is also interesting to note that the final rules differ in each case. We leave you to experiment with random selection of the DATA, as well as expansion of the field of knowledge.

Keeping your expert

Now that your expert has been trained it would be a pity to lose him when the power goes off. However, as the rules are stored in arrays, you could easily write a routine to save them and then reload them for use at a later date.

CHAPTER 7
Fuzzy Matching

Computers are totally logical but our own memory banks are much more unreliable, which can lead to problems when you are trying to recover information on a particular subject. For example English is a very variable language and there are frequently alternative spellings of the same (or very similar) surnames, which can cause difficulties. One way round this problem is to try to match the sound of the word rather than the actual letters in it by means of 'soundex coding', which was originally developed to assist processing of the 1890 census in the USA. This method of coding ensures that similar sounding words have almost the same code sequence. The rules for coding a word are as follows:

1) Always retain the first letter of the word as the first character of the code. From the second letter onward:
2) Ignore vowels (a, e, i, o, u).
3) Ignore the letters w, y, q and h.
4) Ignore punctuation marks.
5) Code the other letters with the values 1–6 as follows:

Letters	Code
bfpv	1
cgjksxz	2
dt	3
l	4
mn	5
r	6

6) Where adjacent letters have the same code only the first one is retained.
7) If length of code is greater than four characters then take first four only.
8) If length of code is less than four characters then pad out to four characters with zeros.

To make this clear here are some examples of soundex coded names:

BRAIN – B650: B is retained, R is 6, A and I are dropped, N is 5 and a zero is added to pad out the code.

CUNNINGHAM – C552: C is retained, U is dropped, both Ns are represented by the single code 5, I is dropped, the third N is represented by 5, G is 2, H and A are dropped, and M is coded as 5 — but the resulting code (C5525) is truncated to four characters.

GORE – G600: G is retained, O is dropped, R is 6, E is dropped and zeros are added to pad the code.

IRELAND – I645: I is retained, R is 6, E is dropped, L is 4, A is dropped, N is 5 and D is 3 — but the resulting code (I6453) is truncated to four characters.

SCOT – S300: S is retained, C is dropped because it is in the same group as S, O is dropped, T is 3 and zero is added to pad the code.

If your name is full of vowels and other rejected letters then you will find that your code is somewhat abbreviated!

HEYHOE – H000: H is retained, all the other letters are rejected (!), and the code is filled up with zeros.

Coding routine

To save all that brainwork let's develop a program which allows you to input a word in English and output it in soundex code (see **Flowchart 7.1**). The first thing to do is to jump to a SET_UP routine which first of all RESTOREs the DATA pointer and then calls SCREEN which sets up a suitable series of screen windows.

```
   10 SET_UP

10000 DEFine PROCedure SET_UP
10010    RESTORE
10020    SCREEN
10030    CODES

10050 END DEFine SET_UP
```

The SCREEN display is divided vertically into two main windows (#1 and #2), with #0 at the bottom reserved for INPUT, and #3 and #4 at the top of the screen used for labels (see **Figure 7.1**).

```
11000 DEFine PROCedure SCREEN
11010    MODE 4
```

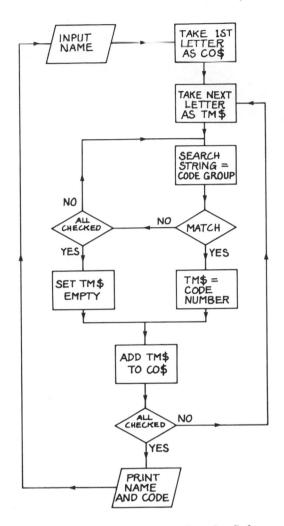

Flowchart 7.1:   Producing a Soundex Code.

```
11020    WINDOW #2,230,186,26,30
11030    BORDER #2,2,6
11040    CSIZE #2,1,0
11050    CLS #2
11060    WINDOW #1,230,186,257,30
11070    BORDER #1,2,4
11080    CSIZE #1,1,0
11090    PAPER #1,5
11100    INK #1,0
11110    CLS#1
```

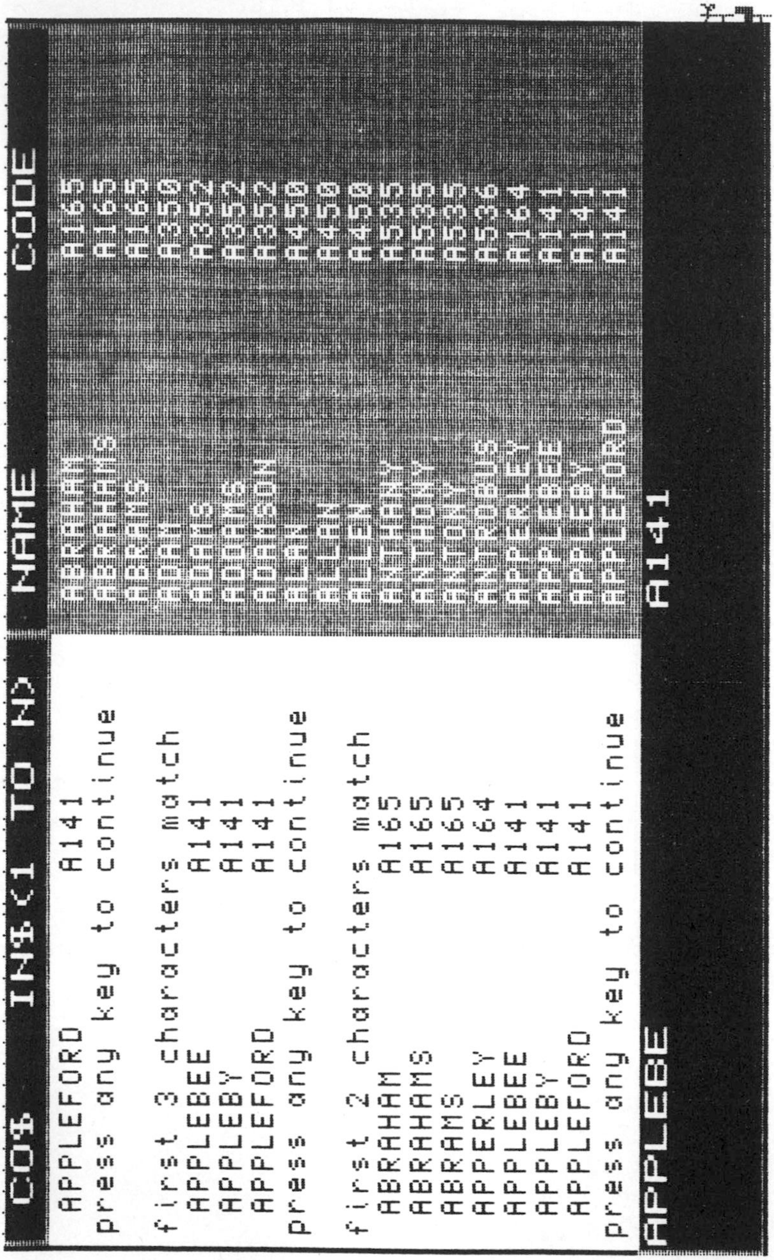

Figure 7.1: Fuzzy Matching.

```
11120    BORDER #0,1,4
11130    CSIZE#0,2,0
11140    CLS #0
11150    OPEN #3,SCR_230X14A257X16
11160    OPEN #4,SCR_230X14A26X16
11170    BORDER #3,1,4
11180    BORDER #4,1,4
11190    CSIZE #3,2,0
11200    CSIZE #4,2,0
11210    PAPER #3,0
11220    PAPER #4,0
11230    INK #3,7
11240    INK #4,7
11250    CLS#3
11260    CLS#4
11270    PRINT #3," NAME","    CODE"
11280    PRINT #4," CO$";"    ";"IN$(1 TO N)";
11290 END DEFine SCREEN
```

The CODES PROCedure reads each group of the retained letters into one element of a soundex code string array, SC$(n). Note that these groups are arranged so that the letters are in the array element corresponding to their code value.

```
12000 DEFine PROCedure CODES
12010    DIM SC$(6,7)
12020    DATA "BFPV","CGJKSXZ","DT","L","MN","R"
12030      FOR N=1 TO 6
12040        READ SC$(N)
12050      END FOR N
12060 END DEFine CODES
```

We can now INPUT the word to be converted, IN$. (A mug-trap is provided for an empty string, but if you want to convert automatically from lower case you can include the GET$ PROCedure described in Chapter 2.)

```
100 REPeat LOOP
110    AT #0,1,2 : INPUT #0,IN$; : IF
         IN$="" THEN LOOP

140 END REPeat LOOP
```

As conversion to the code numbers and compilation of a soundex code string will be required at various points, we will set this process up as a FuNction named COMPILE$. As this is a FuNction we can easily PRINT out the result of passing IN$ to it.

```
120   AT #0,20,2 : PRINT #0, COMPILE$
       (IN$)\\
```

To begin with we must make the coded version of this, CO$, the first letter of the INPUT word (following the first rule above).

```
15000 DEFine FuNction COMPILE$ (IN$)
15010   TM$=IN$(1) : CO$=TM$ : CONVERSION
```

For conversion of each letter to the appropriate code character, we have to check TM$ against each individual letter in each group of letters, SC$(N), to find a match. To check each letter group we have to go round six times, making a search string, SE$, the current soundex code group and using an INSTR routine which checks each letter in the group against TM$ in turn.

```
16000 DEFine PROCedure CONVERSION
16010   LOCal P
16020     FOR P=1 TO 6
16030       SE$=SC$(P)
16040       SP%=TM$ INSTR SE$
```

When the INSTR check has been made we have to determine whether a match has been found to any of the soundex groups, and, if so, to which group. If no match is found then SP% will be set to 0. On the other hand if a match is found then SP% will be set to P which will point to the value of the code group matched. If a match was found (SP%>0) then we convert the value of the loop scanning the code groups, P, to a string, TM$, which replaces our original temporary string.

```
16050         IF SP%>0 THEN TM$=P : RETurn
```

If no match is found in that group, we have to check the next group.

```
16060     END FOR P
```

If no match is found at all then TM$ must contain one of the characters to be ignored so we reset TM$ empty — TM$="".

```
16070    TM$=""
16080 END DEFine CONVERSION
```

We then need to check the other letters of the word, 2 TO LEN(IN$), in turn after first making a temporary string, TM$, equal to the current letter to be translated.

```
15030      FOR N=2 TO LEN(IN$)
15040         TM$=IN$(N)
15050         CONVERSION
```

We can now make the coded string, CO$, equal to the original coded string plus the newly-converted character, TM$, and RETurn the final result when all characters in IN$ have been checked.

```
15080              CO$=CO$&TM$

15110      END FOR N

15140      PRINT #2
15150         RETurn CO$
15160 END DEFine COMPILE$
```

The final converted code will eventually be printed out at the bottom of the screen (next to the INPUT) but it would be instructive to watch how the computer reaches its decision. Adding the following line to the COMPILE$ routine will provide a detailed printout of the state of play during each cycle of the conversion in the lefthand window.

```
15100      PRINT #2," ";CO$,,IN$(1 TO N)
```

If you INPUT the name STEVEN you will get the code S315, by the following route:

CO$	IN$(1 TO N)
S3	ST
S3	STE
S31	STEV
S31	STEVE
S315	STEVEN

However, if you try BRAIN or CUNNINGHAM you will get codes B65 and C55525 respectively.

CO$	IN$(1 TO N)
B6	BR
B6	BRA
B6	BRAI
B65	BRAIN
C	CU
C5	CUN
C55	CUNN
C55	CUNNI
C555	CUNNIN
C5552	CUNNING
C5552	CUNNINGH
C5552	CUNNINGHA
C55525	CUNNINGHAM

The code for BRAIN is too short, and needs padding out with zeros, and the code for CUNNINGHAM is too long and the same codes are repeated one after another for the letter N.

Dealing with the details
To solve the problem of the repetition of the same code for adjacent letters, we need to keep a record of the last temporary string, LT$. We need to make LT$ the code of the first character in IN$ to start with, so that the initial letter is not repeated. As we go through the FOR–NEXT loop we must then compare LT$ with TM$, and if they are the same we must not add TM$ to CO$. Otherwise we need to make LT$ the latest TM$.

```
15020    LT$=TM$

15060         IF TM$<>LT$ THEN
15070            LT$=TM$

15090         END IF
```

Now we can sort out the problem of the code being too short. First of all we check the length of the string, LEN(CO$)<4. If it is too short we add three zeros on to the end and then cut the string back down to the correct size (four characters).

```
15120         IF LEN(CO$)<4 THEN CO$=CO$&"000"
              : CO$=CO$(1 TO 4)
```

Finally if the string is too long then we cut it down to size with CO$(1 TO 4) again (see **Flowchart 7.2**).

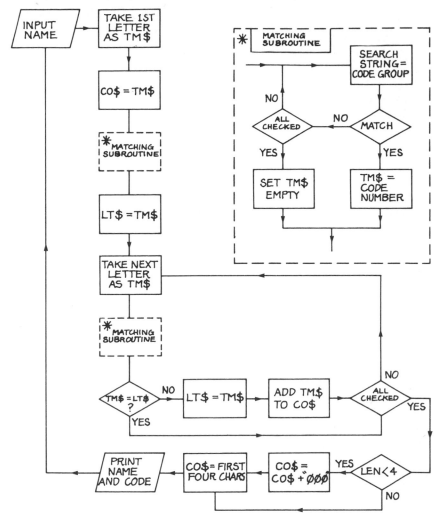

Flowchart 7.2: Dealing with the Details.

```
15130      IF LEN(CO$)>4 THEN  CO$=CO$(1 TO
           4)
```

Matchmaking

Now that we have a reliable method of producing the soundex codes, let's give it something to work on. The first task is to READ a list of names out of DATA statements into a name string array, NA$(N). Our demonstration list only consists of 18 names, but if you want more a quick flick through your local telephone directory should soon solve that problem! Note that the number of words is also stored as NW%, and that this PROCedure is now called from within SET_UP.

```
10040    NAMES

13000 DEFine PROCedure NAMES
13010    LT$="" : NW%=17
13020    DIM NA$(NW%,16) : DIM NC$(NW%,16)
13030    DATA "ABRAHAM","ABRAHAMS","ABRAMS",
         "ADAMS","ADDAMS","ADAMSON","ALAN",
         "ALLAN","ALLEN"
13040    DATA "ANTHANY","ANTHONY","ANTONY",
         "ANTROBUS","APPERLEY","APPLEBEE",
         "APPLEBY","APPLEFORD"
13050     FOR N=0 TO NW%
13060       READ NA$(N)
13070     END FOR N

13120 END DEFine NAMES
```

The whole idea of matching with soundex codes relies on the fact you use the soundex code to make the match before printing the possible words. We therefore have to find the codes for each of the names from the DATA and put these codes into an equivalent string array, NC$(N). However, this is easy as the previously DEFined FuNction COMPILE$ can be re-used to find the soundex code, if NA$(Q) is passed instead of IN$.

```
13080     FOR Q=0 TO NW%
13090       NC$(Q)=COMPILE$ (NA$(Q))
13100       PRINT NA$(Q),NC$(Q)
13110     NEXT Q
```

If you RUN this now you will see all the codes for the DATA produced (on the left window) and displayed (on the right window) before the input request. However, the righthand display is rather ragged, so let's smarten it up by formatting it with a TABLE$ FuNction. This puts the results into two neat columns by adding padding spaces to the righthand end of the strings, and then retaining only the first part of the result.

118

```
13100        PRINT TABLE$(NA$(Q),NC$(Q))

14000 DEFine FuNction TABLE$ (I1$,I2$)
14010   I1$=I1$ & FILL$(" ",16)
14020   I2$=I2$ & FILL$(" ",8)
14030   I1$=I1$(1 TO 16)
14040   I2$=I2$(1 TO 8)
14050      RETurn " "&I1$&I2$
14060 END DEFine TABLE$
```

NAME	CODE
ABRAHAM	A165
ABRAHAMS	A165
ABRAMS	A165
ADAM	A350
ADAMS	A352
ADDAMS	A352
ADAMSON	A352
ALAN	A450
ALLAN	A450
ALLEN	A450
ANTHANY	A535
ANTHONY	A535
ANTONY	A535
ANTROBUS	A536
APPERLEY	A164
APPLEBEE	A141
APPLEBY	A141
APPLEFORD	A141

The only thing we need to do now is to compare the codes and determine which of these names match the code of your input.

```
130   COMPARE

17000 DEFine PROCedure COMPARE

17030      FOR N=0 TO NW%
17040        IF CO$=NC$(N) THEN PRINT #2
             ,TABLE$ (NA$(N),
             NC$(N))
17050      END FOR N

17090 END DEFine COMPARE
```

119

This will only print words with exactly matching soundex codes. For example, if you try entering the name APPLEBE you will get the following response:

APPLEBE   A141

NAME   CODE
APPLEBEE   A141
APPLEBY   A141
APPLEFORD   A141

Although APPLEBE (one E at the end) is not present in the DATA, we have found APPLEBEE AND APPLEBY, as well as APPLEFORD (where the interesting sound at the end has been chopped off).

Partial matching

Notice, however, that APPERLEY has been rejected, even though it sounds quite similar at first. It would therefore be useful if we could also print out partial matches.

This can easily be done by adding an extra FOR–NEXT loop which compares a decreasing section (1 TO M) of the INPUT with decreasing lengths of the stored codes (see **Flowchart 7.3**).

```
17010    FOR M=4 TO 1 STEP -1
17020       PRINT #2,\"first ";M;" characters
            match"\

17040          IF CO$(1 TO M)=NC$(N)(1 TO M)
               THEN PRINT #2,TABLE$ (NA$(N),
               NC$(N))

17060       PRINT #2,"press any key to continue"
17070       DUMMY$=INKEY$(-1)
17080    END FOR M
```

If you now try APPLEBE, you can see the whole range of possibilities.

APPLEBE   A141

first 4 characters match
APPLEBEE   A141
APPLEBY   A141
APPLEFORD   A141
press any key to continue

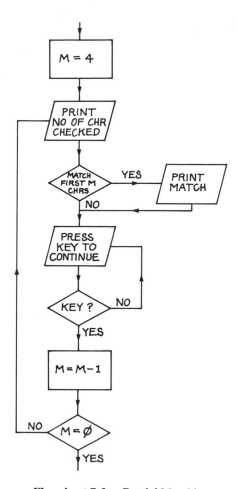

Flowchart 7.3:   Partial Matching.

first 3 characters match
APPLEBEE   A141
APPLEBY   A141
APPLEFORD   A141
press any key to continue

first 2 characters match
ABRAHAM   A165
ABRAHAMS   A165
ABRAMS   A165
APPERLEY   A164
APPLEBEE   A141

121

```
APPLEBY        A141
APPLEFORD      A141
press any key to continue

first 1 characters match
ABRAHAM        A165
ABRAHAMS       A165
ABRAMS         A165
ADAM           A350
ADAMS          A352
ADDAMS         A352
ADAMSON        A352
ALAN           A450
ALLAN          A450
ALLEN          A450
ANTHANY        A535
ANTHONY        A535
ANTONY         A535
ANTROBUS       A536
APPERLEY       A164
APPLEBEE       A141
APPLEBY        A141
APPLEFORD      A141
press any key to continue
```

CHAPTER 8
Recognising Shapes

We normally recognise objects using our senses of sight, sound, taste and feel, whereas of course our basic computer can only obtain information through the keyboard. Whilst it is possible to produce sensors which can be interfaced to your machine to give it another view of the outside world, constructing these requires a reasonable amount of electronic and mechanical knowledge and skill. We will make do instead with a simulation of the action of a light sensor to illustrate how shapes can be recognised.

Let us think for a start about three simple shapes — a vertical line, a square, and a right-angled triangle.

We can recognise these shapes by looking at the pattern they make on an imaginary grid and deciding whether or not there is a point set at each X and Y coordinate.

In the case of the line, only the first X coordinate is used, but all of the Y coordinates. The square is a little more complicated, as all the X coordinates on Y rows 1 and 8 are set, but from Y rows 2 to 7 only the first and last X points are set. Finally the triangle is even more complicated as the slope is produced by incrementing the X axis each time.

Table 8.1:   Decimal Values of Shapes Described in Binary Form.

Y row	line	square	triangle
1	1	255	1
2	1	129	3
3	1	129	5
4	1	129	9
5	1	129	17
6	1	129	33
7	1	129	65
8	1	255	255

One obvious way to describe these particular figures would be to represent each point by a single bit and produce a decimal value for each row in the same way as we did before when we were looking at expert systems (see **Table 8.1**). In fact this type of approach is used to produce the characters which you see on your screen display, the formats for which are stored in memory in just this form. For example, **Figure 8.1** shows how the letter 'A' is built up.

Figure 8.1:   Forming the Letter 'A'.

There are now machines available (optical character readers) which can reverse this process and actually 'read' a printed page by scanning the paper in a grid pattern and measuring whether light is reflected at particular coordinates.

What they actually take in will be a pattern of 'yes' and 'no' for each coordinate and of course this must then be decoded and compared with the patterns for known shapes. The most obvious way to make this comparison would be to consider every point in turn as a binary digit and then convert each row back to a decimal value which could then be compared with a table of known values. However this has the disadvantage that we must actually check every individual point on the grid (64 points).

A branching short cut

A quicker approach relies on the fact that each character can actually be detected by looking at a much smaller number of critical features of the

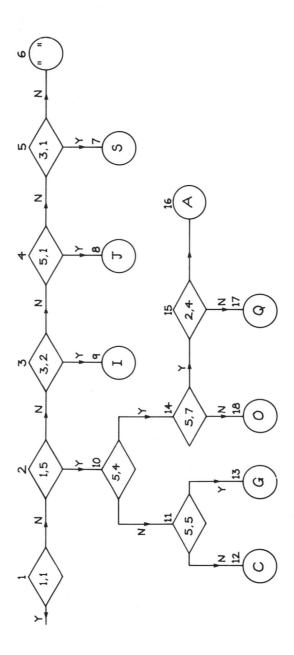

Figure 8.2(a):   Decision Tree for Alphabet.

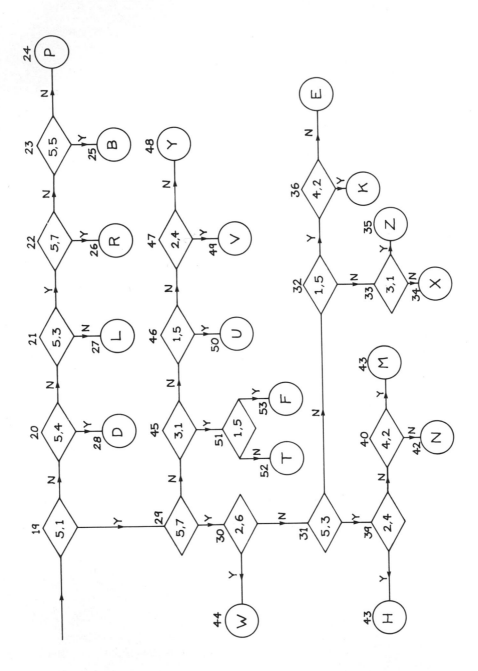

Figure 8.2(b)

pattern. For example, **Figure 8.2** gives a decision tree which will find all the capital letters of the alphabet using only 12 points (see **Figure 8.3**), and it is not even necessary to check all 12 in any particular case. If you follow each of the routes you will see that the maximum number of steps to be followed is 7, and that most letters are found in less than 5 steps (**Table 8.2**). This must obviously be quicker than comparing all 64 points!

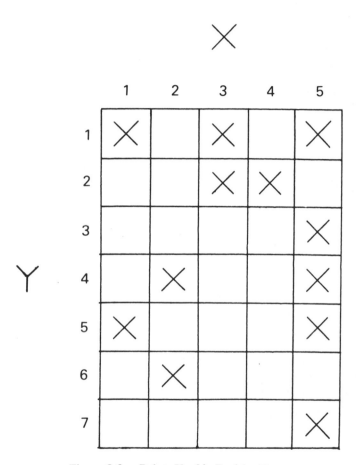

Figure 8.3:   Points Used in Decision Tree.

To demonstrate how this approach works, we will simulate the action of the scanning head by producing a grid on the screen, on which you can construct characters.

The SET_UP routine does the initial housekeeping, starting with the display.

Table 8.2:   Numbers of Steps Required for Recognition of Each Character.

3 steps – I, D
4 steps – L, J, C, G, O, W
5 steps – S, A, Q, R, T, F, U, space
6 steps – P, V, Y, H
7 steps – B, M, N, E, K, X, Z

```
   10 SET_UP

10000 DEFine PROCedure SET_UP
10010    SCREEN

10070 END DEFine SET_UP
```

The SCREEN is cleared and two vertical windows are set up. The left window (#2) is cleared to white, and the right window (#1) to green.

```
11000 DEFine PROCedure SCREEN
11010    MODE 4
11020    PAPER 0
11030    CLS
11040    WINDOW #2,270,200,26,16
11050    BORDER #2,3,7
11060    CSIZE #2,1,0
11070    CLS #2
11080    WINDOW #1,144,200,318,16
11090    BORDER #1,1,7
11100    CSIZE #1,1,0
11110    PAPER #1,5
11120    INK #1,0
11130    CLS #1
11140    BORDER #0,10,0
11150    INK #0,7
11160    CLS #0
11170 END DEFine SCREEN
```

The decision tree is held in a series of linked arrays where NB is the number of branches, LE$(N) holds the names of the letters, C1(N) the X coordinate to be checked next, C2(N) the Y coordinate to be checked

next, N(N) the next element to use if the answer was 'no', and Y(N) the
next element to use if the answer was 'yes'.

```
10020     AT #2,5,10 : PRINT #2,"LOADING DATA
          INTO ARRAY"
10030     TREE
10040     CLS#2



12000 DEFine PROCedure TREE
12010     RESTORE
12020     NB=53 : DIM LE$(NB),C1(NB),C2(NB)
          ,N(NB),Y(NB)
12030       FOR C=1 TO NB
12040         AT #2,15,12 : PRINT #2,C
12050         READ LE$(C) : READ C1(C) :
              READ C2(C) : READ N(C) : READ Y(C)
12060       END FOR C
12070     DATA 0,0,0,2,19
12080     DATA 0,0,4,3,10
12090     DATA 0,2,1,4,9
12100     DATA 0,4,0,5,8
12110     DATA 0,2,0,6,7
12120     DATA "_",0,0,0,0
12130     DATA "S",0,0,0,0
12140     DATA "J",0,0,0,0
12150     DATA "I",0,0,0,0
12160     DATA 0,4,3,11,14
12170     DATA 0,4,4,12,13
12180     DATA "C",0,0,0,0
12190     DATA "G",0,0,0,0
12200     DATA 0,4,6,18,15
12210     DATA 0,1,3,17,16
12220     DATA "A",0,0,0,0
12230     DATA "Q",0,0,0,0
12240     DATA "O",0,0,0,0
12250     DATA 0,4,0,20,29
12260     DATA 0,4,3,21,28
12270     DATA 0,4,2,27,22
12280     DATA 0,4,6,23,26
12290     DATA 0,4,4,24,25
12300     DATA "P",0,0,0,0
```

```
12310    DATA "B",0,0,0,0
12320    DATA "R",0,0,0,0
12330    DATA "L",0,0,0,0
12340    DATA "D",0,0,0,0
12350    DATA 0,4,6,45,30
12360    DATA 0,1,5,31,44
12370    DATA 0,4,2,32,39
12380    DATA 0,0,4,33,36
12390    DATA 0,2,0,34,35
12400    DATA "X",0,0,0,0
12410    DATA "Z",0,0,0,0
12420    DATA 0,3,1,38,37
12430    DATA "K",0,0,0,0
12440    DATA "E",0,0,0,0
12450    DATA 0,1,3,40,43
12460    DATA 0,3,1,42,41
12470    DATA "M",0,0,0,0
12480    DATA "N",0,0,0,0
12490    DATA "H",0,0,0,0
12500    DATA "W",0,0,0,0
12510    DATA 0,2,0,46,51
12520    DATA 0,0,4,47,50
12530    DATA 0,1,3,48,49
12540    DATA "Y",0,0,0,0
12550    DATA "V",0,0,0,0
12560    DATA "U",0,0,0,0
12570    DATA 0,0,4,52,53
12580    DATA "T",0,0,0,0
12590    DATA "F",0,0,0,0
12600 END DEFine TREE
```

A 5×7 GRID array (don't forget the zero elements) is DIMensioned to hold the points set information on the character which we will produce, and the cursor position is set to the top lefthand corner of this (X% = 0, Y% = 0).

```
10050    DIM GRID(4,6)
10060    X%=0 : Y%=0
```

Key prompts are displayed on the lefthand screen and then we are ready to use the EDITOR to design our character.

```
20    REPeat CHARACTER
30      PRINT #2,\"SPACEBAR to set point"
40      PRINT #2,\"F1 to erase point"
50      PRINT #2,\"F2 to clear screen"
60      PRINT #2,\"F3 to decode"
70      EDITOR

90    END REPeat CHARACTER
```

A block representation of the contents of the GRID array, with a flashing cursor to show your position, is produced in the righthand window (#1) by the EDITOR. The loop sets a block at the current coordinates (X%,Y%) to colour 2 (red), and then checks IF the corresponding GRID array element contains 1 (ie GRID (X%, Y%) is TRUE). If 1 is found then this block is set to colour 0 (black). Alternatively, ELSE sets the block back to colour 4 (green), so that there is no lasting effect. The rate of flashing is controlled by the delay value in the INKEY$(N) check, and the sequence repeats until a key is pressed.

```
13000 DEFine PROCedure EDITOR
13010   REPeat LOOP
13020     BLOCK 28,28,(X%*28),(Y%*28),2
13030       IF GRID(X%,Y%) THEN
13040         BLOCK 28,28,(X%*28),(Y%*28),0
13050           ELSE
13060             BLOCK 28,28,(X%*28),(Y%*28
                    ),5
13070         END IF
13080     A$=INKEY$(5)
13090       IF A$="" THEN END REPeat LOOP
```

When a key is pressed, the CODE of this key is taken and used in a series of IF–THEN tests. The X and Y coordinates are updated according to movement of the cursor keys and if the spacebar is pressed the colour of the current screen position is set to black *and* the corresponding GRID element is set to 1. If you make a mistake then Function key 1 erases the current position by resetting the colour to green, and resets the GRID element to 0. Note that checks have to be included to prevent movement beyond the edges of the grid.

```
13100     A=CODE(A$)
13110       IF A=192 AND X%>0 THEN X%=X%-1 :
```

```
                    END REPeat LOOP
13120               IF A=200 AND X%<4 THEN X%=X%+1 :
                    END REPeat LOOP
13130               IF A=208 AND Y%>0 THEN Y%=Y%-1 :
                    END REPeat LOOP
13140               IF A=216 AND Y%<6 THEN Y%=Y%+1 :
                    END REPeat LOOP
13150               IF A=32 THEN GRID(X%,Y%)=1 :
                    BLOCK 28,28,(X%*28),(Y%*28),0 :
                    END REPeat LOOP
13160               IF A=232 THEN GRID(X%,Y%)=0 :
                    BLOCK 28,28,(X%*28),(Y%*28),4 :
                    END REPeat LOOP
```

If your character design becomes a complete disaster then Function key 2 clears the screen in window #1, and then resets all the points in the GRID to 0.

```
13170               IF A=236 THEN
13180                 CLS #1
13190                   FOR C=0 TO 4
13200                     FOR M=0 TO 6
13210                       GRID(C,M)=0
13220                     END FOR M
13230                   END FOR C
13240        END REPeat LOOP
13250          END IF
```

Finally Function key 3 RETurns to the READER PROCedure which decodes your design, or else the program loops back to the keycheck.

```
13260               IF A=240 THEN RETurn
13270          END REPeat LOOP
13280 END DEFine EDITOR


   80        READER
```

In the READER PROCedure, the design produced is checked against the recognised patterns (see **Flowchart 8.1**). The array pointer, AP, is first set to 1 so that the search is started from the beginning. X and Y coordinates are read from the C1(AP%) and C2(AP%) elements pointed

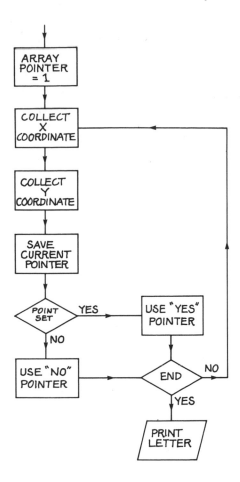

Flowchart 8.1:   READER PROCecure.

to, and the last position, LP%, pointer set equal to the current array pointer, AP%. The point colour, PC, at these coordinates is now determined by looking into the appropriate GRID array element. If this contains 1, then this point has been set and the 'yes' pointer, Y(AP%), must be followed. If any other value is found then the 'no' pointer, N(AP%), is followed. In either case a check is now made to see whether the element pointed to contains a 0 (which indicates the ultimate end of a branch), which shows that a character has been found. If so, the appropriate letter LE$(LP%) is printed in window #0, and the display is held until a key is pressed, when a new cycle is initiated. As long as a higher value than 0 is found, this must be another branch point and so the program loops back and picks up the new values of C1(AP%) and

C2(AP%). To allow you to see which points have been checked these BLOCKS are set to red as they are found. Any points which were set but not tested will remain black.

```
14000 DEFine PROCedure READER

14020    AP%=1
14030      REPeat PIXEL_CHECK
14040        X%=C1(AP%) : Y%=C2(AP%) :
             LP%=AP%
14050        PC%=GRID(X%,Y%)
14060          IF PC% THEN AP%=Y(AP%) :
               ELSE AP%=N(AP%)

14080          IF AP% THEN
14090            BLOCK 28,28,(X%*28),(Y%*
                 28),2
14100      END REPeat PIXEL_CHECK
14110          END IF
14120          CSIZE #0,3,1 : AT #0,6,0 :
               PRINT #0,"CHARACTER IS ";LE$
               (LP%); : CSIZE #0,0,0
14130          PRINT #2,\\"PRESS A KEY TO
               CONTINUE"
14140          A$=INKEY$(-1)
14150          CLS#0 : CLS #1 : CLS #2
14160 END DEFine READER
```

So that you can see which part of the tree was actually followed, add these modifications which will print out the sequence of branches followed along the tree.

```
14010    PRINT #2,\"X axis","Y axis",
         "point","next"
14070        PRINT #2,\X%,Y%,PC%,AP%;
```

The disadvantage of this more rapid method (of only checking critical points) is that it will make a mistaken match if it encounters a shape that is not on the tree, whereas if all points are checked then no match will be found in such a case. Early optical character readers would only accept a single particular typeface, but the latest machines not only accept different styles of type, but actually learn the recognition rules for themselves by means of a built-in expert system. You teach these by showing them a few pages of text and then entering these same characters via the keyboard. However we feel that it will still be a long time before anyone can produce a machine that can read *our* handwriting!

CHAPTER 9
An Intelligent Teacher

Another place where artificial intelligence can be particularly useful is in teaching programs. It is all very well having a program which tests a student's knowledge at random, but this is not how real human teachers work. As well as asking the questions, they keep an eye on the progress of the students, increase the difficulty of the questions as experience increases, and test them more rigorously on the types of problems with which they are having difficulties. For example, if a child takes a test involving addition, subtraction, multiplication and division, but only gets the division questions wrong, then it follows that the child should be given more division questions in the future to provide more practice.

Let's have a look at how we can introduce these 'human' qualities into a teaching program.

Questions and answers
We need to create random numbers to be used in the first question, which we will make an addition. Using RND(0 TO 10) will give numbers between 0 and 10.

```
  10 SCREEN
  20    REPeat QUESTION
  40       A%=RND(0 TO 10)
  50       B%=RND(0 TO 10)

10000 DEFine PROCedure SCREEN
10010    MODE 4
10020    CLS #0 : CLS  #1 : CLS #2
10030 END DEFine SCREEN
```

The computer adds these together and then goes on to an INPUT and CHECKing PROCedure.

```
  60       C%=A% + B%
  70       CHECK
```

First of all, CHECK must print the question and then INPUT your answer, IP%.

```
1000  DEFine PROCedure CHECK
1010    PRINT \A%;"+";B%;"=";
1020    INPUT IP%
```

Your answer must then be checked. If the answer, C%, is the same as your answer then CORRECT is printed, ELSE 'WRONG' is printed followed by the correct answer, and then the next question is asked.

```
1030    IF C%=IP% THEN
1040      PRINT \"CORRECT"
1050        ELSE PRINT \"WRONG, THE CORRECT
                ANSWER WAS ";C%
1060    ENDIF
1080 END DEFine CHECK

 280    END REPeat QUESTION
```

Not a number?

If you experiment with this simple routine, you will find that it crashes if you enter a letter in place of a number (deliberately or accidentally). It would be a much more friendly teacher who refused to accept anything other than a number as INPUT, so we will use a GET PROCedure instead of that simple INPUT request. This INPUTs a string (IP$), rather than a number, and first checks that the string is not empty (RETURN alone pressed). It then checks that the CODE of each character in the string (IP$(N)) is a numeral (CODE between 42 and 56) before converting IP$ to a simple variable (IP%) by coercion.

```
1020      GET
2000 DEFine PROCedure GET
2010   INPUT IP$
2020     IF IP$="" THEN GET
2030       FOR N=1 TO LEN(IP$)
2040         IF CODE(IP$(N)) <43 OR CODE(IP$(N)
             >57 THEN
2050           PRINT " ENTER A NUMBER!!  ";
2060           GET
2070         END IF
2080       END FOR N
```

```
2090    IP%=IP$
2100 END DEFine GET
```

Alternative rules

The other three rules of arithmetic (subtraction, multiplication and division) can be easily dealt with in the same way if we replace the '+' sign in line 1010 by a sign string, SG$, which we can set to the appropriate character at the time. At the same time, as RND(0 TO 10) is common to all the calculations, we might as well DEFine this as a FuNction called PICK which RETurns an appropriate number.

```
1010    PRINT \A%; SG$; B%; "=";


3000 DEFine FuNction PICK
3020    RETurn RND(0 TO 10)
3030 END DEFine PICK


 40     A%=PICK
 50     B%=PICK
 60     C%=A%+B% : SG$="+"
 70     CHECK
100     A%=PICK
110     B%=PICK
120     C%=A%-B% : SG$="-"
130     CHECK
160     A%=PICK
170     B%=PICK
180     C%=A%*B% : SG$="*"
190     CHECK
220     A%=PICK
230     B%=PICK
240     C%=A%/B% : SG$="/"
250     CHECK
```

Dividing by zero

As it stands, the program can crash if B% happens to be 0 when a division is selected. This can be simply fixed by always adding 1 on to B%, in this case:

139

```
230      B%=PICK+1
```

Deleting decimals

We are using integer variables to keep us to round numbers, but of course a division may still produce a fractional answer, which you cannot enter correctly as IP% will be rounded down, eg:

$3/2 = 1.5$

but the program will accept 1, 1.5, 1.9 or any other number between 1 and 1.999. . . as correct.

To avoid producing decimals, A% needs to be a multiple of B%. To achieve this we calculate B% first and make A% equal to B% multiplied by a random number between 0 and 10.

```
220      B%=PICK+1
230      A%=PICK*B%
```

Keeping a score

Now that we have the test itself working we need to consider how to keep a score. The simplest thing is to increment a tries variable, TR%, each time the GET PROCedure is used, and to increment a score variable, SC%, each time a correct answer is obtained.

```
10 SCREEN : TR%=0 : SC%=0

1040      PRINT \"CORRECT" : SC%=SC%+1

2090   IP%=IP$ : TR%=TR%+1
```

Your current performance can now be shown by a SCORE PROCedure called at the end of CHECK.

```
1070      SCORE

4000 DEFine PROCedure SCORE
4010   PRINT "YOUR SCORE IS ";SC%;"/";TR%
4020 END DEFine SCORE
```

If you prefer the score as a percentage then amend line 4010 as follows:

```
4010   PRINT "YOU HAVE HAD ";(SC%/TR%)*100;
       "% CORRECT"
```

How many questions?

The program will now ask one question of each type in sequence, ad infinitum. We can limit this by defining the number of questions, NQ%, as a variable.

```
10 SCREEN : TR%=0 : SC%=0 : NQ%=32
```

Each time a question is asked, NQ% is decreased by 1: when NQ% = 0 the test ends (after eight questions of each type have been answered).

```
2090    IP%=IP$ : TR%=TR%+1 : NQ%=NQ%-1

3010    IF NQ%=0 THEN PRINT "32 QUESTIONS
        ASKED"
```

Shifting the emphasis

If we are going to bias the questions in favour of areas of difficulty, we need to keep a record of performance in each individual area. We therefore need separate variables for each type of question (AD% for addition, SU% for subtraction, MU% for multiplication, and DI% for division). These variables are defined in terms of one eighth of the total number of questions to be asked, NQ%.

```
10 SCREEN : TR%=0 : SC%=0 : NQ%=32 :
   AD%=NQ%/32 : SU%=NQ%/32 : MU%=NQ%/32
   : DI%=NQ%/32
```

Now if the correct answer, C%, is the same as your answer, IP%, then an increment variable, IN%, is set to −1, CORRECT is printed, and the routine returns. Otherwise IN% is set to 1 and WRONG is printed followed by the correct answer.

```
1040       PRINT \"CORRECT" : IN%=-1
1050       ELSE PRINT \"WRONG, THE CORRECT
           ANSWER WAS ";C% : IN%=1
```

IN% is added to the appropriate individual number of questions variable — AD%, SU%, MU% or DI% — on returning from CHECK, producing an increase in this value if the answer was wrong, or a decrease if the answer was right.

```
 70      CHECK : AD%=AD%+IN%

130      CHECK : SU%=SU%+IN%

190      CHECK : MU%=MU%+IN%

250      CHECK : DI%=DI%+IN%
```

Now we add a test to see whether all the questions of a particular type have not been correctly answered (eg AD%>0, see **Flowchart 9.1**). If all questions of a type have been correctly answered then no more of this type are asked as this section is jumped over.

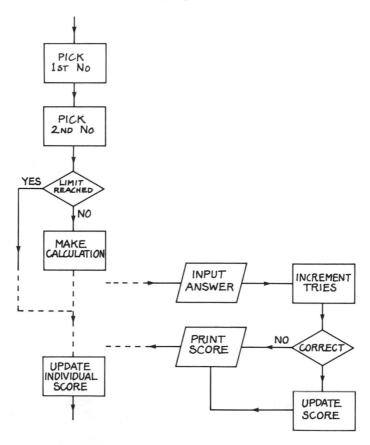

Flowchart 9.1:   Intelligent Teacher.

```
30          IF AD%>0 THEN

80          END IF
90          IF SU%>0 THEN

140         END IF
150         IF MU%>0 THEN

200         END IF
210         IF DI%>0 THEN

260         END IF
```

If the appropriate number of each type has been answered correctly —
AD% = 0, SU% = 0, MU% = 0, DI% = 0 — then the program ends.

```
270    IF AD%+SU%+MU%+DI%=0 THEN PRINT
       "4 QUESTIONS OF EACH TYPE CORRECT"
```

Notice that you are no longer asked questions about areas in which you
have correctly answered four questions without making any errors. If you
make a mistake then AD% (etc) will be increased, and therefore you will
have to answer more than this number correctly before AD% reaches 0.

Degrees of difficulty

How about making the questions easier or harder according to how well
you are doing (ie the values of AD%, SU%, MU%, and DI%)? So far
the current values of A% and B% have always been between 0 and 10, as
they were produced by RND(0 TO 10). We now need to bias the numbers
produced for the questions towards higher values, if you are correct, and
lower values if you are incorrect. At the same time we must ensure that
you do not produce negative values if your performance is abysmal.

To start with, we need to modify the PICK FuNction so that the current
value of the 'number of questions to be asked in each group' pointer
(AD%, SU%, MU% or DI%) is passed to it as X%.

```
40          A%=PICK(AD%)
50          B%=PICK(AD%)

100         A%=PICK(SU%)
110         B%=PICK(SU%)
```

```
160        A%=PICK(SU%)
170        A%=PICK(SU%)

220        B%=PICK(DI%)+1
230        A%=PICK(DI%)
```

3000 DEFine FuNction PICK(X%)

The 'worst case' will be if you get all the questions wrong in the last group. In this case only four questions will be asked on the first three groups, leaving $32-(3*4) = 20$ questions to be asked on the last group. In addition we must remember that X% (eg AD%) starts at a value of 4, so that the maximum value of X% which could be obtained is $20+4 = 24$.

We therefore set up a weighting variable, WT%, which is calculated by subtracting three times the number of questions to be asked in each group ($3*AD\%$) from the total number of questions (NQ%) and adding back on the number of questions in the group AD% at the start.

$$WT\% = NQ\% - (3*AD\%) + AD\%$$

This is more simply expressed as:

$$WT\% = NQ\% - (2*AD\%)$$

```
10 SCREEN : TR%=0 : SC%=0 : NQ%=32 :
   AD%=NQ%/32 : SU%=NQ%/32 : MU%=NQ%/32 :
   DI%=NQ%/32 : WT%=NQ%-(2*AD%)
```

We now replace the fixed value of 10 by the difference between WT% and X%, by modifying the calculation in the PICK FuNction.

3020   RETurn RND(0 TO (WT%-X%))

To begin with, WT% = 24 and X% = 4 so numbers between 0 and 20 will be selected. If a correct answer is given, then X% is reduced to 3 and numbers between 0 and 21 will be chosen. After four correct answers, X% will not change (for this type of question) as it will have reached 0 and the line will be skipped. The last values will therefore be between 0 and 23.

But if the first answer is incorrect, X% will increase by 1 and the range of numbers produced reduced by 1 (0–19). In the 'worst case', X% will be increased 20 times to 24 and (WT%−X%) will fall to zero for both A% and B% (so you should be able to solve that particular problem!).

What about words?

Although the example above deals solely with mathematical problems, there is absolutely no reason why the same technique cannot be used in dealing with more detailed textual questions and answers.

CHAPTER 10
Of Mice and Men

Mankind has been fascinated by mazes for centuries and the difficulties involved in finding the way out of (or to the centre of) a maze have featured prominently in mythology. More recently the theme has been taken up by the enthusiastic band of 'mouseketeers' who send their electronic micromice as their champions to do battle against the unknown. Whilst some may feel that these activities are trivial, we are sure that they would not object too much if somebody else was sent to check for radiation after a nuclear accident, or to explore the surface of some alien planet in their place!

Although short-range direct control of devices is possible, and a video link can allow an operator to 'see' his way, the delays involved in long-distance transmission pose considerable problems. It is of little value to see a picture showing that your multimillion pound exploratory probe is about to fall into a Martian crevasse if it has already fallen by the time you receive the picture! Autonomous intelligent devices will therefore always have their place. Although any real exploratory robotic device must be fitted with suitable sensors, dependent upon its environment and activities, and will require some reliable form of motive power, with our QL alone we can at least simulate some of the problems involved in finding your way around.

Setting the scene

To begin with we set up a screen with three windows. On the right (#1) we will show the actual maze, on the left (#2) the contents of the MOUSE BRAIN are displayed, and at the bottom (#0) we have the current time and status.

```
10 SCREEN

10000 DEFine PROCedure SCREEN
10010    MODE 4
10020    WINDOW #2,230,200,25,15
10030    BORDER #2,1,4
10040    PAPER #2,7
```

```
10050     INK #2,0
10060     CSIZE #2,1,0
10070     CLS #2
10080     WINDOW #1,230,200,258,15
10090     BORDER #1,1,4
10100     PAPER #1,0
10110     INK #1,7
10120     CSIZE #1,1,0
10130     CLS #1
10140     PAPER #0,0
10150     INK #0,0
10160     CSIZE #0,2,0
10170     CLS #0
10180     PAPER #0,7
10190     PRINT #0,"   MOUSE BRAIN
               MAZE        "
10200 END DEFine SCREEN
```

Making the maze

We now need to produce a maze to travel through. Although we could
generate one randomly it is rather more fun to design your own, and it
makes it easier to create tests to determine which particular types of
situation cause confusion. The actual maze is contained within a 37 by 33
array, but a copy of the contents of each array element is also displayed on
window #1. Here each array element is represented in the window by a 6
by 6 pixel BLOCK, and before we start we will show the centre of the
maze (18,16) as a green (colour 4) BLOCK. The start position is set in the
top left corner at X% = 1, Y% = 1.

```
20 DESIGN

11000 DEFine PROCedure DESIGN
11010    DIM MAZE(37,33)
11020    X%=1 : Y%=1
11030    BLOCK 6,6,(18*6),(16*6),4
```

As long as no key is pressed, we loop around flashing a non-destructive
cursor, which alternates between green (colour 4) and the present colour
in the current maze coordinates.

```
11040       REPeat LOOP
11050           BLOCK 6,6,X%*6,Y%*6,4
```

```
11060      BLOCK 6,6,X%*6,Y%*6,MAZE(X%,Y%)
11070      A$=INKEY$(2)
11080        IF A$="" THEN END REPeat LOOP
```

When a key is pressed, the four cursor directions are checked. As long as you remain within set limits in the array the X and Y coordinates are updated, and the screen cursor moves (without leaving a trail).

```
11090      A=CODE(A$)
11100        IF A=192 AND X%>1 THEN X%=X%-1 :
             END REPeat LOOP
11130        IF A=200 AND X%<35 THEN X%=X%
             +1 : END REPeat LOOP
11160        IF A=208 AND Y%>1 THEN Y%=Y%-1
             : END REPeat LOOP
11190        IF A=216 AND Y%<31 THEN Y%=Y%
             +1 : END REPeat LOOP
```

To form the maze we need to mark out a path in the maze array for the mouse to follow. We also show this on the screen as white (colour 6) BLOCKs. So that it is easy to alter the maze by swapping white BLOCKs for black (0), we DEFine a PATH PROCedure to which we can pass a parameter indicating the colour to be used. Remember that both the actual maze and the screen display must be updated.

```
12000 DEFine PROCedure PATH (COLOUR)
12010    MAZE(X%,Y%)=COLOUR
12020    BLOCK 6,6,X%*6,Y%*6,COLOUR
12030 END DEFine PATH
```

White BLOCKs are produced by pressing CTRL and an arrow key, and black erasing BLOCKs by pressing ALT and an arrow key.

```
11110      IF A=193 AND X%>1 THEN PATH 0
           : X%=X%-1 : END REPeat LOOP
11120      IF A=194 AND X%>1 THEN PATH 6
           : X%=X%-1 : END REPeat LOOP
11140      IF A=201 AND X%<35 THEN PATH 0
           : X%=X%+1 : END REPeat LOOP
11150      IF A=202 AND X%<35 THEN PATH 6
           : X%=X%+1 : END REPeat LOOP
```

```
11170          IF A=209 AND Y%>1 THEN PATH 0
               : Y%=Y%-1 : END REPeat LOOP
11180          IF A=210 AND Y%>1 THEN PATH 6
               : Y%=Y%-1 : END REPeat LOOP
11200          IF A=217 AND Y%<31 THEN PATH 0
               : Y%=Y%+1 : END REPeat LOOP
11210          IF A=218 AND Y%<31 THEN PATH 6
               : Y%=Y%+1 :  END REPeat LOOP
```

Should your maze start to look like a disaster area, then pressing SHIFT and F1 will RUN the program so that you can start from scratch again!

```
11220          IF A=234 THEN RUN
```

Finally SHIFTed F2 will RETurn from DESIGN so that the mouse can start his search. (Note that the only condition to be satisfied in the maze is that the start point ($X\% = 1$, $Y\% = 1$) must be connected to the centre in some way.)

```
11230          IF A=238 THEN RETurn
11240     END REPeat LOOP
11250 END DEFine DESIGN
```

Finding the route

We can now send our mouse into action looking for the cheese in the centre of the maze. We need to give him a memory, which will be the same size as the maze array, set him the start position (1,1), and reset the clock with SDATE, so that we can time his progress.

```
30    REPeat RESTART

40       DIM MEMORY(37,33) : X%=1 : Y%=1

60       SDATE 1984,0,0,0,0,0
```

The movement of the mouse falls within a loop (see **Flowchart 10.1**). The first action in this is to PRINT the last five characters of DATE$ (ie the minutes and seconds part). Note that you cannot slice DATE$ itself, but must convert it to the temporary variable D$ first.

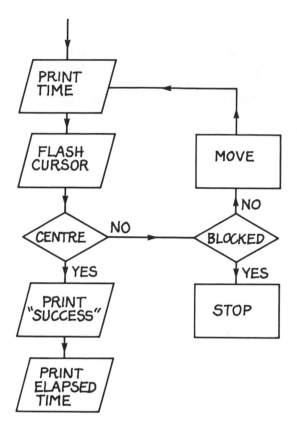

Flowchart 10.1:   Starting Movement.

```
70        REPeat MOVEMENT
80          D$=DATE$
90          D$=D$(16 TO)
100         AT #0,16,0 : PRINT #0,D$

180       END REPeat MOVEMENT
```

The array element at the start coordinates in the MEMORY is set to green (colour 4), and a flashing cursor on window #2 in the corresponding position is produced by the TRACK PROCedure. This takes three parameters (X and Y coordinates and the colour to be used for the BLOCK).

```
110          MEMORY(X%,Y%)=4
120          TRACK X%,Y%,0
130          TRACK X%,Y%,MEMORY(X%,Y%)


1000 DEFine PROCedure TRACK (X1,Y1,C)
1010    BLOCK #2,6,6,(X1*6),(Y1*6),C
1020 END DEFine TRACK
```

A bull's eye?

We can easily check whether the centre has been reached by checking the appropriate coordinates (18,16). When (or maybe that should be IF) the centre is reached, then the journey time is reported, and you have three options. Pressing 'N' RUNs the program so that you can design a new maze. Pressing 'C' clears the screen on window #2 and then returns you to RESTART for another attempt at the same maze (as only the MEMORY array, and not the MAZE array, is reset). Pressing any other key RESTARTs on the same maze without clearing the screen, so that any differences in the points which are checked in the next attempt are more obvious.

```
140              IF X%=18 AND Y%=16 THEN CENTRE


2000 DEFine PROCedure CENTRE
2010    PRINT #0,"  HE REACHED THE CENTRE OF
        THE MAZE"\"     IN ";D$(1 TO 2);"
        MINUTES AND ";D$(4 TO 5);" SECONDS"
2020    A$=INKEY$(-1)
2030      IF A$="N" THEN RUN
2040      IF A$="C" THEN CLS #2 : END REPeat
        RESTART
2050    END REPeat RESTART
2060 END DEFine CENTRE
```

Which way?

The mouse must take a look to see where it is possible to move. The next position to be examined is determined by adding X and Y Decision values (XD% and YD%) on to the current coordinates. To begin with, we will set XD% to 0 and YD% to 1, so that the mouse will always try to move down.

```
50      XD%=0 : YD%=1

150           IF MAZE(X%+XD%,Y%+YD%)=0 THEN
              STOP

170           X%=X%+XD% : Y%=Y%+YD%
```

RUN the program, draw a simple vertical line, and start the mouse by pressing SHIFT F2. You will see that he moves down until he reaches the end of the line, when he STOPs. So far so good but we now have to decide what he should do when the next position does contain 0.

Coping with corners

Your first thought might be to reverse the direction if a wall is hit (inverting XD% and YD% by multiplying them by −1) but of course that would only send the mouse shuttling back and forth along the line ad infinitum. If he is to be able to make a turn to a new heading then he must check around to find out more about his surroundings. Four FuNctions are defined to cope with each of the four possible directions (left, right, up, down). Each of these works in basically the same way, using an UNKNOWN PROCedure to find out what is in the next possible position. So far we have only looked at the maze and have not put any information into the mouse memory. As long as nothing has been put into a MEMORY location then this will still be 0. We must therefore copy the appropriate maze information into MEMORY, as well as making a TRACK to show that we have looked here. If the location has already been checked then UNKNOWN has no effect. Now if any of the direction FuNctions find an unchecked MEMORY location then we RETurn immediately without CHECKing the other possibilities. This means that LEFT has priority over RIGHT, which has priority over UP, which has priority over DOWN. Note that this means that the mouse will always make the same decisions, and that XD% and YD% are only updated if the Colour Code variable (CC) is matched, indicating a pathway is present (see **Flowchart 10.2**).

```
150 DUMMY=CHECK

3000 DEFine FuNction CHECK
3020    CC=6
3060       IF LEFT THEN RETurn 0
3070       IF RIGHT THEN RETurn 0
```

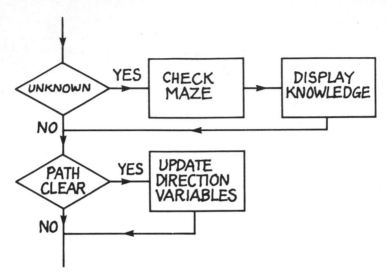

Flowchart 10.2:   Coping with Corners.

```
3160     IF UP THEN RETurn O
3170     IF DOWN THEN RETurn O
3240   RETurn -1
3250 END DEFine CHECK


4000 DEFine PROCedure UNKNOWN (X1,Y1)
4010   IF MEMORY(X1,Y1)=0 THEN
4020     MEMORY(X1,Y1)=MAZE(X1,Y1)
4030     TRACK X1,Y1,MEMORY(X1,Y1)
4040   END IF
4050 END DEFine UNKNOWN


5000 DEFine FuNction LEFT
5010   UNKNOWN X%-1,Y%
5020     IF MEMORY(X%-1,Y%)=CC THEN XD%=-1 :
         YD%=0 : RETurn -1
5030   RETurn O
5040 END DEFine LEFT
```

```
6000 DEFine FuNction RIGHT
6010    UNKNOWN X%+1,Y%
6020       IF MEMORY(X%+1,Y%)=CC THEN XD%=1 :
            YD%=0 : RETurn -1
6030    RETurn 0
6040 END DEFine RIGHT

7000 DEFine FuNction UP
7010    UNKNOWN X%,Y%-1
7020       IF MEMORY(X%,Y%-1)=CC THEN XD%=0 :
            YD%=-1 : RETurn -1
7030    RETurn 0
7040 END DEFine UP

8000 DEFine FuNction DOWN
8010    UNKNOWN X%,Y%+1
8020       IF MEMORY(X%,Y%+1)=CC THEN XD%=0 :
            YD%=1 : RETurn -1
8030    RETurn 0
8040 END DEFine DOWN
```

If you try that out with a winding pathway such as that shown in **Figure 10.1**, you will see that only LEFT and RIGHT are actually checked most of the time, as the program RETurns before UP and DOWN are reached.

Cutting the checks

As things are, LEFT, RIGHT and UP must all be checked before DOWN, whereas it would be more sensible if we reduced the amount of checking done by introducing a bit more logic. Only LEFT and RIGHT need to be CHECKed when XD% is 0 (ie the mouse was already moving UP or DOWN), and only UP and DOWN CHECKed when YD% was 0 (ie he was already moving LEFT or RIGHT, see **Flowchart 10.3**).

```
3030       IF XD%=0 THEN
3060              IF LEFT THEN RETurn 0
3070              IF RIGHT THEN RETurn 0
3120       END IF
3130       IF YD%=0 THEN
3160              IF UP THEN RETurn 0
3170              IF DOWN THEN RETurn 0
3220       END IF
```

Figure 10.1: Coping with Corners.

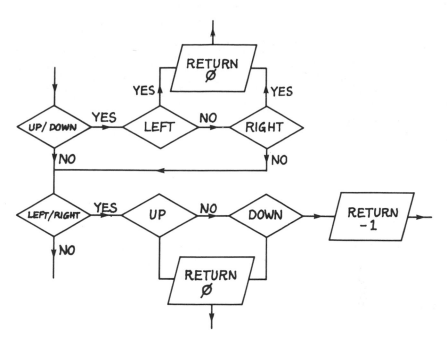

Flowchart 10.3:   Cutting the Checks.

Jinxing at junctions

Our mouse will now move round corners OK, but if he reaches a junction then he will always move LEFT or UP, if they are possible, as these possibilities are always checked first. Such predictable behaviour can get him going round in circles, so it would be better if we introduced random selection from the two possible directions in each case, so that he does not always give the same priority. LR% (LEFT–RIGHT) and UD% (UP–DOWN) variables are chosen at random as 1 or 2, and used to reverse the order in which the directions are checked (see **Flowchart 10.4**).

```
3000 DEFine FuNction CHECK
3020    CC=6
3030      IF XD%=0 THEN
3040        LR%=RND(1 TO 2)
3050         IF LR%=1 THEN
3060            IF LEFT THEN RETurn 0
3070            IF RIGHT THEN RETurn 0
3080         ELSE
3090            IF RIGHT THEN RETurn 0
```

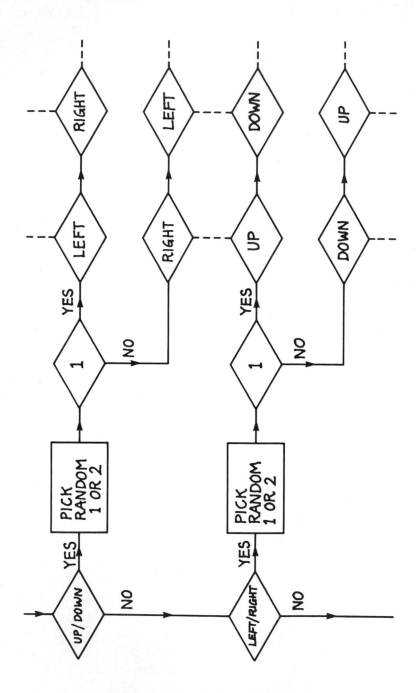

Flowchart 10.4:   Jinxing at Junctions.

```
3100                IF LEFT THEN RETurn 0
3110            END IF
3120        END IF
3130        IF YD%=0 THEN
3140            UD%=RND(1 TO 2)
3150            IF UD%=1 THEN
3160                IF UP THEN RETurn 0
3170                IF DOWN THEN RETurn 0
3180            ELSE
3190                IF DOWN THEN RETurn 0
3200                IF UP THEN RETurn 0
3210            END IF
3220        END IF
3240    RETurn -1
3250 END DEFine CHECK
```

If you try that out several times on a maze containing a square (eg **Figure 10.2**) then you will notice that now the same path is not always followed.

Backtracking

Now IF all the checks are negative, AND the next maze position contains 0 (indicating a wall rather than an unchecked position) then the mouse's only alternative is to go into reverse (multiplying the current XD% and YD% variables by -1 — see **Flowchart 10.5**).

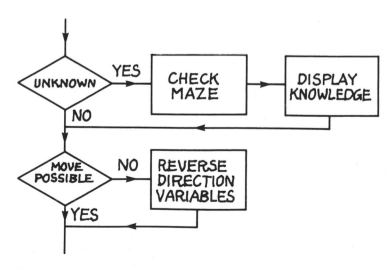

Flowchart 10.5:   Backtracking.

159

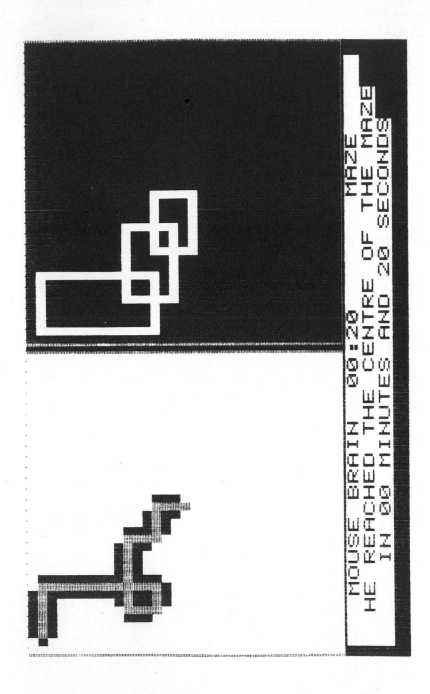

Figure 10.2:   Jinxing at Junctions.

```
150 UNKNOWN X%+XD%,Y%+YD%
160 IF CHECK AND MAZE(X%+XD%,Y%+YD%)=0
    THEN XD%=XD%*-1 : YD%=YD%*-1
```

He will now reverse when a dead end is reached, and continue to check until an alternative pathway is found.

Where no mouse has gone before

It seems sensible to give a higher priority to parts of the maze which have not already been visited, as the odds in favour of success are biased towards the unknown.

In the program so far the areas he has not visited, but which are valid paths, are marked as white (colour 6), and those visited once are marked in the MEMORY as green. We can arrange so that when the mouse backtracks the trail colour is changed from green to red. This is easily done by adding a FOR loop which alters the value of CC in the CHECK routine. Now, as the loop decrements by 2 each time it repeats, white is checked for first, followed by green (4) and, as a last resort, red (2). Once the first match is found we RETurn so that we now have effectively produced the colour priority white > green > red.

```
3020    FOR CC=6 TO 2 STEP-2
3230    END FOR CC
```

Speed merchant?

Although the progress of the mouse is now 'slow but sure', you might consider that it would be better not to bother to make detailed checks on the surroundings IF the path ahead was shown to be clear (ie colour 6). Adding the following line speeds the mouse up considerably, as he now only makes checks when that is absolutely necessary (**Figure 10.3**).

The disadvantages with this approach are that he becomes more predictable and that he will always go straight on at a junction when that is possible. In particular, side branches will not be found without back-tracking. How important that is in specific situations depends on the deviousness of your maze, which of course is up to you!

```
3010    IF MEMORY(X%+XD%,Y%+YD%)=6 THEN RETurn 0
```

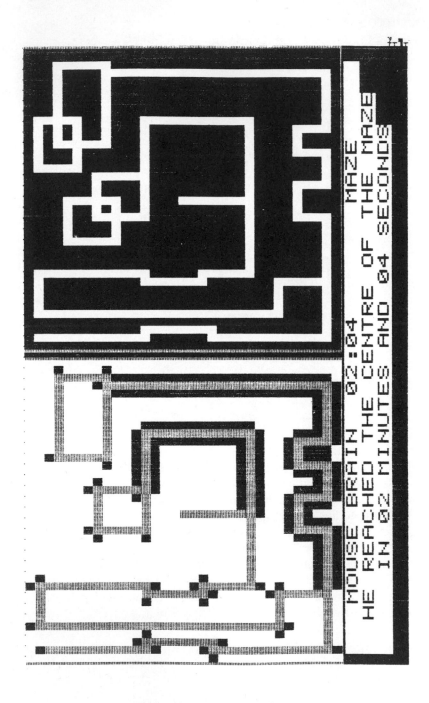

Figure 10.3: Speed Merchant.

CHAPTER 11
Intelligent Use of Archive

The ARCHIVE intelligent database program included with the QL is a powerful tool for manipulating records and extracting information. It is a good example of a 'state of the art' intelligent program, but to use it most effectively you must understand clearly how it operates.

Now whole books could (and no doubt will) be written on ARCHIVE alone, so we will concentrate here on two aspects only. The first of these is how to use the commands to extract the required information correctly, and the second is how you could produce a more user-friendly shell for the 'British Standard Idiot' to use.

Start by loading the ARCHIVE program from microdrive with:

lrun mdv1_boot

Now a DIRectory of microdrive 1 should show the sample database file included with the program (GAZET_DBF).

dir "mdv1_"

(Note that quotation marks are needed to access the microdrive from within ARCHIVE.)

To make life easy we will use this GAZETteer database to explore the potential of ARCHIVE, so first of all we need to activate it with:

look "mdv1_gazet"

At this point, DISPLAY will show the layout and the first record in the file (see **Figure 11.1**).

display

To move on through the file you can use:

next

and if you are browsing through the file then repeated typing of 'next' can

163

```
Logical name      :  main
country$          :  AFGHANISTAN
continent$        :  ASIA
capital$          :  KABUL
languages$        :  PUSHTU,DARI
currency$         :  AFGHANI
pop               :  19.5
gdp               :  110
area              :  657
```

Figure 11.1:   First Record.

be avoided by pressing F5, which repeats the last text in the keyboard buffer, and then ENTER. Although this feature is of limited value in this particular case, it is a boon when a long sequence of commands are involved.

To retrace your steps use:

back

Or for major leaps:

first

or:

last

Finding a match

The simplest matching command available is FIND, which searches all fields of a record for a match with the input string.

For example:

find "europe"

will display the record for ALBANIA, which is the first occurrence of EUROPE.

It is important to notice that the lower case input (europe) was matched with the upper case (EUROPE), as FIND is case-independent.

To find the next match with the same string, CONTINUE is used rather than NEXT.

Thus:

continue

will produce the record for AUSTRIA.

One feature of FIND is that it looks for a match with any part of the record, and takes no account of surrounding characters. This can sometimes be a problem:

find "asia"
continue

produces first AFGHANISTAN but then AUSTRALIA, which is of course in AustralASIA rather than simply ASIA.

On the other hand, this can be useful if you only want to match part of a record. For example 'languages' often contains the name of more than one language, but you will still find matches with any part of this.
Thus:

find "english"
continue
continue
continue

will eventually retrieve the BOTSWANA record where languages$ is 'ENGLISH, SETSWANA', rather than simply 'ENGLISH'.

Another good example would be finding which countries use some form of dollar ($) as currency.

find "$"

picks AUSTRALIA (with the AS$) as the first match.

Sometimes it is advantageous to deliberately truncate an input word to obtain all required matches. If you compare:

find "english"

with

find "engl"

you will see that the latter produces significantly more matches.

Searching specifically
SEARCH is a more specific, but also more powerful, command which

requires that a specified condition is satisfied. It acts only on specified fields, and is case-dependent, so that:

search continent$ = "asia"

finds no matches but:

search continent$ = "ASIA"

does, whilst:

search continent$ = "AMERICA"

finds nothing as 'AMERICA' is always preceded by some qualifying letter such as 'N'.

Although you cannot search to find which countries use the dollar as the unit of currency (as the dollar string is usually embedded) you can easily search to determine whether a number is greater or less than a specified value. Thus whilst SEARCH is basically more exact it allows you to be less precise in some ways!

Hence:

search area <2

gives

HONG KONG (1)
MARTINIQUE (1)

and

search area >10000

produces only

U.S.S.R (22402)

Strings can be compared as well as numbers:

search country$ >"C"

gives

CAMEROUN

(the first country beginning with a character sequence further up in alphabetical order than the letter specified, 'C').

More than one condition to be satisfied may be specified. For example how many countries in Africa use French as their sole language?

search continent$ = "AFRICA" and
languages$ = "FRENCH"

BENIN
CENTRAL AFRICAN REP.
CHAD
COMORO IS.
CONGO
GUINEA
IVORY COAST
MALI
REUNION
TOGO

What about asking which of those use the CFA FR as currency as well? The obvious way to do that is to tack another condition on:

search continents$ = "AFRICA" and
languages$ = "FRENCH" and
currency$ = "CFA FR"

CENTRAL AFRICAN REP.
CHAD
COMORO IS.
CONGO
IVORY COAST
TOGO

Selecting records
A more effective way of dealing with this type of problem may be to SELECT subsets of records. The total number of records in the GAZET file can be found by:

print count ( )

where the answer is 152.
    You can select countries in Africa only with:

select continent$ = "AFRICA"

Now

print count ( )

gives only 49, and the system acts as if only those records existed. Hence:

search languages$ = "FRENCH"

will now find the French-speaking-only countries in Africa, or you could select just these with:

select languages$ = "FRENCH"
print count ( )

leaving only ten countries in the file. (There is no reason why this selection cannot be done in a single step.)

Putting things in order

If you look at the list of French-speaking African countries above, you will see that they are in alphabetical order. This is purely fortuitous as the whole GAZET file was originally set in alphabetical order by country, but this ORDER can be easily modified.

Thus:

order area;a

puts them into ascending order by area as

COMORO IS.
REUNION
TOGO
BENIN
GUINEA
IVORY COAST
CONGO
CENTRAL AFRICAN REP.
MALI
CHAD

and

order capital$;a

puts them into ascending order according to the name of the capital (with ABIDJAN in the IVORY COAST top of the list).

Whether selection or searching is quicker really depends on what particular information you are trying to extract.

To retrieve the whole file use:

reset

Partial matches

In one of the examples above we SELECTed the African countries which have French as their sole language — but what about those who have both French and other languages? Remember that FIND is not specific — so why not select the countries in AFRICA, as before, and then find 'FRENCH'.

select continent$ = "AFRICA"
find "FRENCH"
continue

Using PROCedures

So far we have only scratched the surface of the potential of ARCHIVE as we have only used direct commands, which have simply located and displayed entire matching records. However, using the PROCedure editor we can tailor more impressive sequences for specific tasks. To enter the editor type:

edit

and when you are prompted for a PROCedure name enter:

cont1

and then the following PROCedure lines which carry out an automatically repeated FIND.

```
proc cont1
  cls
  input "which continent? ";a$
```

169

```
find a$
while found()
  print country$;"   ";
  continue
  endwhile
endproc
```

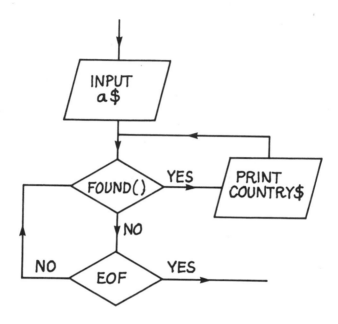

Flowchart 11.1:   PROC cont1.

A search string (a$) is input in reply to the 'which continent?' question, and a FIND for this is continued while FOUND( ) is true (see **Flowchart 11.1**). Now FOUND( ) is zero when FIND was unsuccessful, providing a suitable loop-ending test. Notice that we have specified that only country$ is printed, rather than the whole record, so that only the requested information is displayed. Once the PROCedure is entered you can press ESC to return to ARCHIVE and then run your new PROCedure by simply entering its name:

cont1

When the prompt appears enter 'asia' when a list showing only the names of countries in ASIA will appear — but note that AUSTRALASIA has also been found.

To restrict the match to 'ASIA' you can search instead. The only line that needs to be changed is:

find a$

which becomes

search continent$ = a$

Of course only upper case will now be matched, which can be rather a nuisance. One way round this is always to convert your input into upper case, and as this is a common requirement we might as well define it as a new PROCedure called GET. Enter the editor as before and then use F3 and 'N' to create a new PROCedure.

```
proc get
  input a$
  let a$=upper(a$)
endproc
```

The input line in CONT1 now needs to be replaced by:

print "which continent? "; : get

if both 'ASIA' and 'asia' are to be accepted. To go back to your old CONT1 PROCedure, press ESC followed by SHIFT and TABULATE, and then edit the line.

A more friendly (inter)face

So far you have to type the string to be matched exactly as it appears in the record — but it would be more user-friendly if you could be rather vaguer. Who knows, you might even be able to convince your sceptical relations that computers are worth talking to!

We will define a new PROCedure called TELL, which provides an outer 'shell' so that the user never has to worry about the nitty-gritty details of what is actually being done within ARCHIVE (**Flowchart 11.2**).

A major feature is that it uses an INSTR search of your input against keywords to try to find out what you want, rather than simply accepting it as given.

Now when you use TELL you are prompted to make an input, which can contain anything you like. This is checked for key sequences of

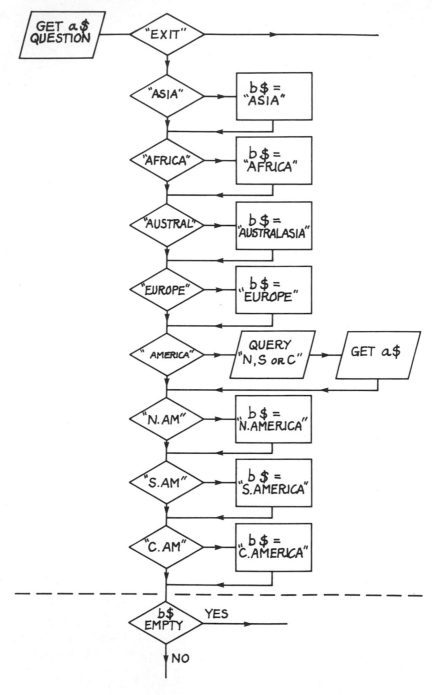

Flowchart 11.2(a):   Proc tell (i).

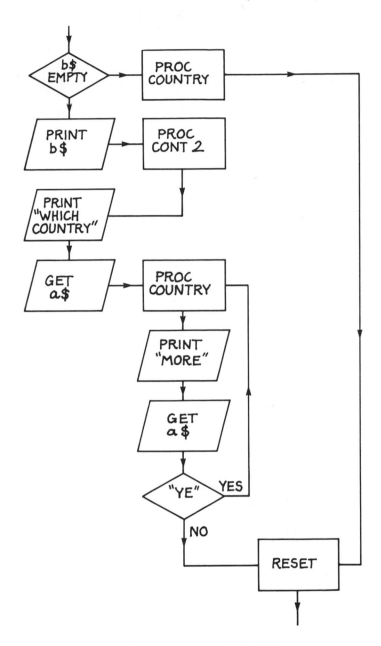

Flowchart 11.2(b):   PROC tell (ii).

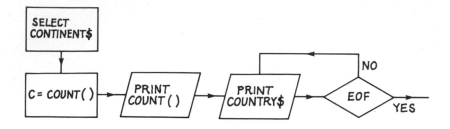

Flowchart 11.2(c): PROC cont2.

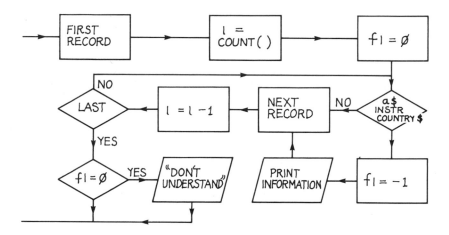

Flowchart 11.2(d): PROC country.

characters, such as ASIA, AFRICA, AUSTRAL, and EUROPE. If you now enter any sentence containing one of these key phrases which describe continents, a search will be made for the appropriate match.

Thus:

ASIA
ASIAN
ASIATIC
AFRICA
AFRICAN
AUSTRALIA
AUSTRALIAN
AUSTRALASIA
AUSTRALASIAN
EUROPE
EUROPEAN

```
WORLD INFORMATION

PLEASE ENTER YOUR QUESTION


? PLEASE WILL YOU GIVE ME SOME INFORMATION ABOUT
  AMERICA

DO YOU MEAN
N.AMERICA
S.AMERICA
OR C.AMERICA
N.AMERICA
N.AMERICA

There are 2 countries in N.AMERICA

CANADA      U.S.A

Which country would you like to know more about?
CANADA


CANADA is in N.AMERICA
It has a population of 23.1 million,
spread over 9976000 sq km
(a population density of 2.32/sq km)
The capital is OTTAWA
and the currency is the CAN.$

Do you wish to have any
more information about N.AMERICA
YES PLEASE

Which country would you like to know more about
U.S.A.


U.S.A. is in N.AMERICA
It has a population of 215.3 million
spread over 9363000 sq km
(a population density of 22.99/sq km)
The capital is WASHINGTON
and the currency is the $

Do you wish to have any
more information about N.AMERICA
NO
```

Figure 11.2:   Sample Printout from TELL PROCedure.

will all be accepted.

In the case of AMERICA a more mug-trapped approach is used as the GAZET file divides this into three distinct areas, which must be specified precisely. Note that this depends on finding a space before AMERICA.

If a continent name is not found (b$ = "") then a check is made to see whether the input is the name of a country by the COUNTRY PROCedure, which checks for a match between your input and all the country$ variables in the file. Note that this uses an odd 'logic' as your input may contain any number of words, whereas the variable in the record is only a single phrase. Thus we look for country$ in your input (a$) rather than vice versa.

If a match is found then a number of variables are picked from this record and presented neatly embedded in text. Note that this information also contains the DERIVED population density figure which was not in the actual record. The WHILE L (ie count( )) loop will check all records in the file, so that you can ask about more than one country at a time, but the INKEY( ) check gives you an easy way out if you can't stand the graunching sound from the microdrives any longer. If no match is found then you are advised of this and you return to the calling PROCedure.

Where the name of a continent is found the CONT2 PROCedure is called, which selects the records of all those countries in this area, and prints out their names. You are now asked 'which country would you like to know more about', and the COUNTRY PROCedure is used to find this as before. The WHILE R loop allows you to repeat your searches on this continent.

Figure 11.2 gives a sample printout of the program.

This approach is obviously rather more friendly, but you can see that the hard work has had to be done in advance, and that all the INSTR checking inevitably slows things down. Perhaps you would like to try adding more facilities to the program so that you can check more than one field at a time.

ARCHIVE TELL PROCedure

```
proc tell
  reset
  mode 0,6
  let dummy=-1
  while dummy
    cls
    print
    print "WORLD INFORMATION"
    print
```

```
print "PLEASE ENTER YOUR QUESTION"
print
let b$=""
print
print "? ";
get
if a$="EXIT"
  print "BYE FOR NOW"
  let dummy$=getkey()
  mode 1,6
  reset
  return
  endif
if instr(a$,"ASIA")>0
  let b$="ASIA"
  endif
if instr(a$,"AFRICA")>0
  let b$="AFRICA"
  endif
if instr(a$,"AUSTRAL")>0
  let b$="AUSTRALASIA"
  endif
if instr(a$,"EUROPE")>0
  let b$="EUROPE"
  endif
if instr(" "+a$," AMERICA")>0
  print
  print "DO YOU MEAN?"
  print "N.AMERICA"
  print "S.AMERICA"
  print "OR C.AMERICA?"
  print
  get
  endif
if instr(a$,"N.AM)>0
  let b$="N.AMERICA"
  endif
if instr(a$,"S.AM)>0
  let b$="S.AMERICA"
  endif
if instr(a$,"C.AM)>0
  let b$="C.AMERICA
  endif
```

```
  if b$<>""
    print b$
    cont2
    let r=-1
    while r
      print
      print "Which country would you
      like to know more about? "
      get
      print
      country
      print "Do you wish to have any"
      print "more information about ";b$
      get
      if instr(a$,"YE")=0
        let r=0
        endif
      endwhile
    else
    country
    endif
  let dummy$=getkey()
  reset
  endwhile
endproc
```

ARCHIVE CONT2 PROCedure

```
proc cont2
  select continent$=b$
  let c=count()
  print
  print "There are ";c;" countries in";b$
  print
  while c
    if c/4=int(c/4)
      print
      endif
    print country$;"   ";
    next
    let c=c-1
    endwhile
  endproc
```

ARCHIVE COUNTRY PROCedure

```
proc country
  first
  let l=count()
  let fl=0
  while l
    if INSTR(a$,country$)>0
      let fl=-1
      print
      ink 4
      print country$;" is in ";continent$
      print "It has a population of ";pop;
      " million,"
      print "spread over ";area;"000 sq
      km"
      print "(a population density of ";
      print str(pop/(area/1000),0,2);
      "/sq km)"
      print "The capital is ";capital$
      print "and the currency is the ";
      print currency$
      ink 7
      endif
    next
    let l=l-1
    if inkey()<>""
      return
      endif
    endwhile
  if fl=0
    ink 2
    paper 7
    print "I don't understand what you
    mean"
    ink 7
    paper 0
    endproc
```

CHAPTER 12
A Naturally Expert Salesman

In the previous chapters we have dealt from first principles with various aspects of artificial intelligence, but in this final chapter we have linked together many of these individual ideas into a single complete program. The original intelligent program was the famous ELIZA, which was a pseudo-psychiatrist program written to send up a particular style of psychiatric therapy, but we have resisted the temptation to follow this lead any further and have opted instead to produce a synthetic replacement for the computer salesman.

Although ELIZA-type programs which will hold a 'conversation' with you are not uncommon, this particular program is rather unusual in that it combines processing of natural language with an expert system to produce a result which should both understand your natural language requests and make suggestions which take into account your requirements, the strengths and weaknesses of particular machines in 20 different areas, and a number of hard commercial facts like cost and profit margin!

Enough words and values have already been included to make the program interesting, but you can easily customise it by adding your own ideas to the DATA. (We take no responsibility for the values included so far, which are for demonstration purposes only, or the views on particular machines expressed by the program.) The program itself basically follows the methods described earlier in the book and the functions of the various PROCedures, FuNctions, variables and arrays are given in **Table 12.1**.

Table 12.1(a):   Variables and Arrays.

SIMPLE VARIABLES

QP%	no. of question sentences
Q%	no. of questions
R%	no. of rules
OB%	no. of objects
AJ%	no. of adjectives
AV%	no. of adverbs
LI%	no. of likes

DL%	no. of dislikes
NJ%	no. of negative adjectives
NV%	no. of negative adverbs
HM%	no. of cheap/expensive
BB%	bank balance
CO%	no. of computers
FE%	no. of features
CT%	no. of cost ratings
CS%	no. of cost suggestions
EX%	no. of excuses
HI%	no. of high price suggestions
LO%	no. of low price suggestions
LD%	like/dislike
TC%	total cost
TP%	total profit
OF%	object flag
NP%	negative/positive
M%	marker
OM%	object marker
S1%	AND position
S2%	BUT position
CM%	comma position
SP%	search position
ST%	search start
PH%	selected question phrase
IS%	search position
RU%	rule update value
XX%	cheap/expensive
TX%	selected excuse
PT%	selected credit warning
TS%	cost of most expensive match
BS%	cost of least expensive match
HI%	most expensive match
LO%	least expensive match
SE%	most/least
SL%	cost phrase selector

ARRAYS

OB$(OB%,10)	objects
AJ$(AJ%,6)	adjectives
NJ$(NJ%,7)	negative adjectives

AV$(AV%,6)	adverbs
NV$(NV%,6)	negative adverbs
LI$(LI%,7)	likes
DL$(DL%,7)	dislikes
Q$(Q%,20)	question objects
QP$(QP%,16)	question sentences
CR(Q%)	cost rate
PR(Q%)	profit rate
IC(Q%)	total cost
IP(Q%)	total profit
HM$(HM%,20)	cheap/expensive
R(R%)	desire rule
CO$(CO%,30)	computer names
FE(CO%,FE%)	feature names
C(CT%)	cost ratings
CS$(CS%,100)	cost suggestions
EX$(EX%,100)	excuses
HI$(HI%,100)	high messages
LO$(LO%,100)	low messages

Table 12.1(b):   PROCedures and FuNctions.

PROCEDURES

SCREEN	set windows
TITLE	prints title
SET_UP	READs DATA, sets variables
PICK_QUESTION	selects question phrase (PH$)
LOOK_AT	looks for '@' marker in PH$
LOOK_AND	looks for '&' marker in PH$
JOIN_1	forms the question with the question objects at the end
JOIN_2	forms the question with the question objects embedded
AND_OR_BUT	updates the rules depending upon the word preceding the AND_OR_BUT in your input
YES_PRESENT	updates the rules if YES_PRESENT in your input
NO_PRESENT	updates the rules of NO_PRESENT in your input

NT_PRESENT	updates the rules if NT_PRESENT in your input
DOUBLE_NEGATIVE	checks for a DOUBLE_NEGATIVE in your input
LIKES	checks for LIKES verbs in your input
DISLIKES	checks for DISLIKES verbs in your input
OBJECTS	checks for OBJECTS in your input
ADVERBS	checks for ADVERBS (positive)
NEGATIVE_ADVERBS	checks for NEGATIVE_ADVERBS
ADJECTIVES	checks for ADJECTIVES (positive)
NEGATIVE_ADJECTIVES	checks for NEGATIVE_ADJECTIVES
CHEAP_EXPENSIVE	prints cheap or expensive message
RULE_UPDATE	updates rules
COST_PROFIT	calculates total cost and profit
SPENDING	compares with bank balance
PICK_COMPUTER	selects matching computer

FUNCTIONS

FIND_slash	searches for a slash '/' in PH$
FIND_ask	searches for an asterisk '*' in PH$
FIND_comma	searches for a comma ',' in IN$
FIND_AND	searches for 'AND' in IN$
FIND_BUT	searches for 'BUT' in IN$

Making conversation

The format of the program is that you are asked for your views on each of a number of possible features in turn (the exact wording of the question being PICKed at random from a selection of available QUESTION phrases). Note that the keyword or phrase is inserted into the sentence where necessary and that the correct conjugation is applied, by FIND_ slash, LOOK_at, LOOK_and, FIND_ask, JOIN_1 and JOIN_2.

The screen display is divided into five horizontal windows (**Figure 12.1**) which are dedicated to specific purposes. Window #0, at the bottom,

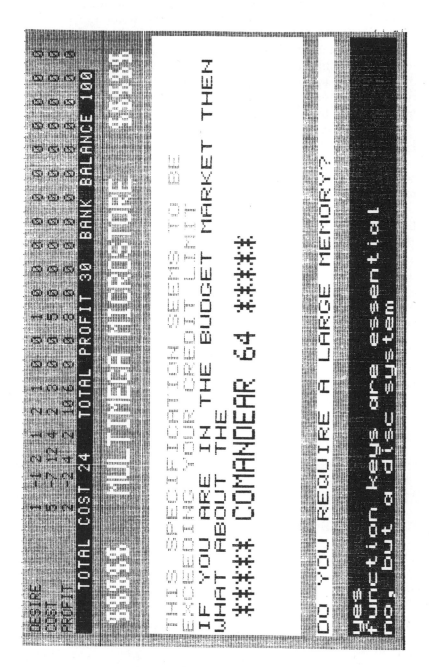

Figure 12.1:   Workings of Salesman's Mind.

receives your input sentences, which are entered in response to the prompting questions which appear on the small window (#3) just above it. Above this is the largest window (#1) on which a whole series of relevant comments appear. Window #4 simply contains an advertisement for the 'Multimega Microstore', whilst finally the top window (#2) displays at least part of the contents of the salesman's brain, to show the rules on which he is basing his judgement. Of course this may give you more insight into a salesman's motives than usual.

Your input is examined in detail for a series of keywords, and a DESIRE RULE array is updated according to your requests. (You actually see the rule arrays being updated in the top screen window.) Note that many of the keywords are truncated so that one check can be made for a number of similar words, and a test is included to check that the matching string is at the start of a word, to reduce mismatches (eg LIKE in DISLIKE). If you are obsessed with one particular feature (eg 16-BIT PROCESSOR) then the salesman does not take you too seriously as this is obviously a 'buzz word' gleaned from the last month's issue of 'People's Computer News'.

The simplest test is whether there is YES_PRESENT or NO_PRESENT which add or subtract 1 from the DESIRE RULE for that feature, and if you mention the name of the OBJECTS (eg GRAPHICS) then a further 1 is added to the DESIRE RULE. In addition, using 'positive' ADJEC-TIVES or ADVERBS also adds to this rule, whilst a NEGATIVE_ADJECTIVE or NEGATIVE_ADVERB subtracts from this rule. Separating the words into different classes allows you to make more than one change to this rule at the same time.

Thus:

YES	adds 1
YES BASIC	adds 2
YES BASIC NECESSARY	adds 3
YES GOOD BASIC NECESSARY	adds 4

Whilst:

NO	subtracts 1

and

NO MEMORY	subtracts 2

Furthermore verbs are grouped as LIKES and DISLIKES: the latter reverse the action of the rest of the words.
Thus:

I DETEST MACRODRIVES   subtracts 1

Both NO_PRESENT and NT_PRESENT are recognised and most DOUBLE_NEGATIVEs are interpreted correctly.
Thus:

I DON'T LIKE SOUND   subtracts 2

I DON'T DISLIKE SOUND   adds 2

If anything appears at the start of a sentence and is followed by a comma then FIND_COMMA usually cuts it off and it is effectively ignored.
Thus:

NO, I DON'T WANT GOOD SOUND   subtracts 3

The exception is when AND_OR_BUT are included, when both parts of the sentence are acted on independently.
Thus if the question is:

DO YOU WANT GRAPHICS?

and the answer is:

NO, BUT I WANT GOOD SOUND

then 1 is subtracted from the graphics rule and 2 added to the sound rule.
If the program does not find any keywords in the input then it politely asks you to try again:

PARDON, EXCUSE ME BUT . . .

The program can only cope with one feature at a time so if you try to ask for SOUND and GRAPHICS, for example, at the same time, you will get a request for a repeat of the question.

HANG ON — ONE THING AT A TIME

However it is possible to make comments about single features that you are not being asked about at the time, and these entries will still update the rules (as in the BUT example above).

187

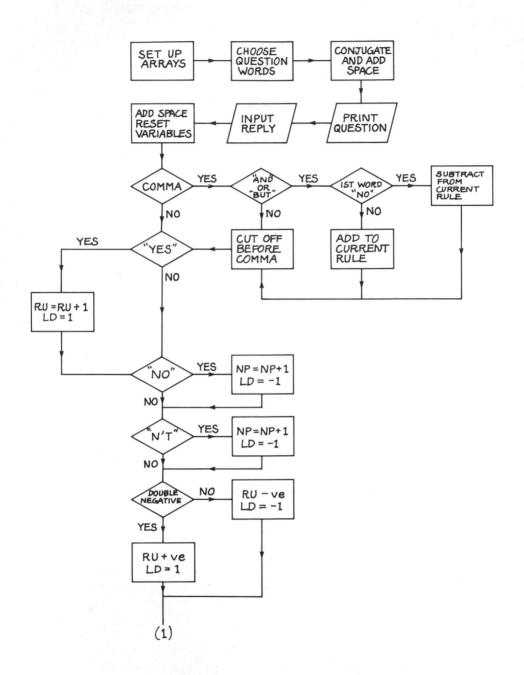

Flowchart 12.1(a): Computer Salesman.

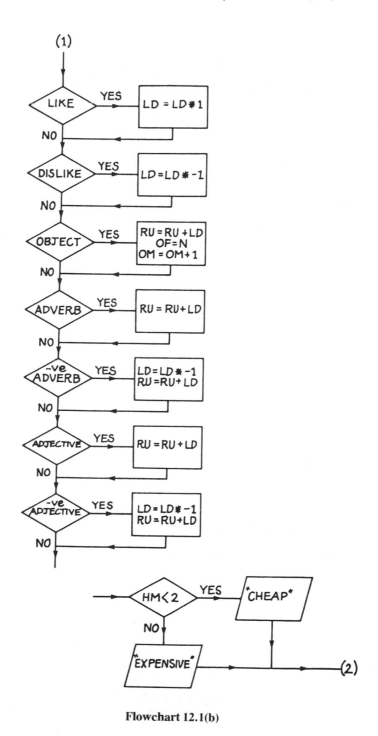

Flowchart 12.1(b)

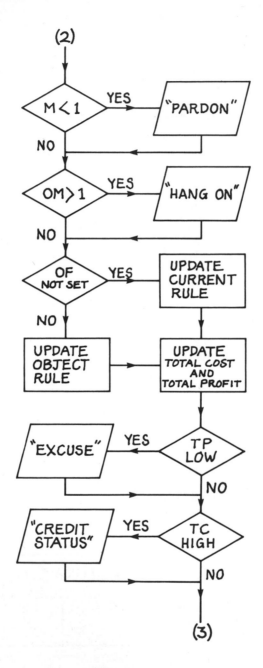

Flowchart 12.1(c)

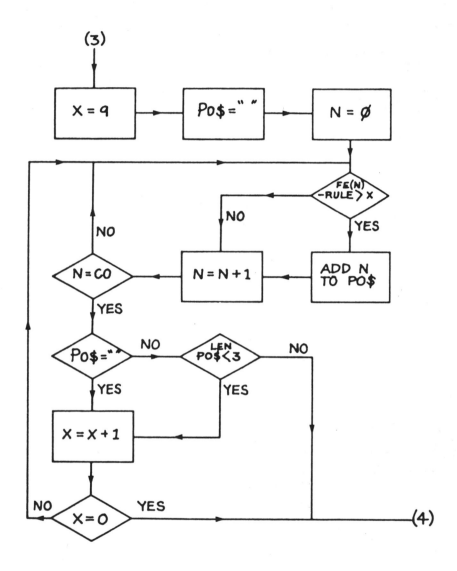

Flowchart 12.1(d)

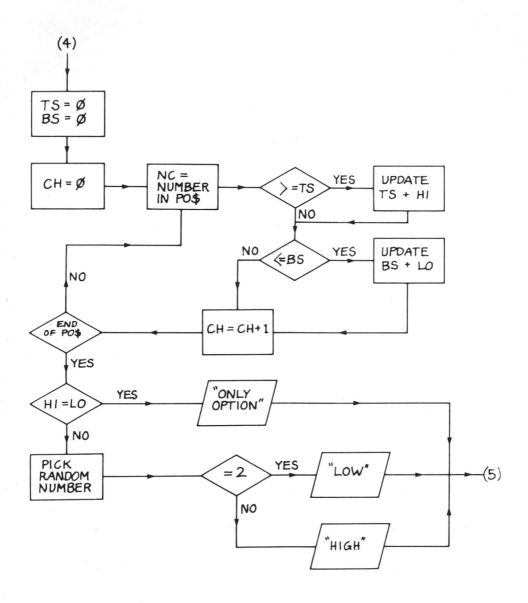

Flowchart 12.1(e)

Decisions

Once the input has been decoded as far as possible we move to RULE_
UPDATE. In addition to the DESIRE RULE array there are two other
arrays which are linked to this. The first is the COST RULE, which gives
an indication of the cost of this particular option, and the second is the
PROFIT RULE which indicates to the salesman how much effort it is
worth putting into selling this feature. The values for these last two arrays
are produced by multiplying the content of the corresponding rule array
element by factors entered originally in the DATA (see **Table 12.2**)
where the format is:

(phrase describing feature, cost, profit)

eg EXPANDABILITY,2,9

indicates that the cost of including EXPANDABILITY is quite low (2)
but that it carries the potential for high profits, through sale of ex-
pansions.

Table 12.2:   Cost and Profit Margin of Features.

NO.	FEATURE	COST	PROFIT
1	GOOD BASIC	5	2
2	GRAPHICS	7	2
3	SOUND	6	2
4	A GOOD KEYBOARD	4	2
5	FUNCTION KEYS	1	5
6	A LARGE MEMORY	3	6
7	A TAPE INTERFACE	2	2
8	MACRODRIVES	2	4
9	DISCS	5	8
10	EXTENSIVE SOFTWARE	0	9
11	A CARTRIDGE PORT	1	6
12	A JOYSTICK PORT	1	7
13	AN ASSEMBLER	2	1
14	A CENTRONICS PORT	2	5
15	AN RS232 PORT	2	6
16	EXPANDABILITY	2	9
17	NETWORKING	3	4
18	A 16-BIT CPU	1	7
19	MULTITASKING	5	5
20	GOOD SERVICE	1	9

After each input the salesman considers the consequences of your requests. First of all he looks to see if your SPENDING on your requirements exceeds a certain proportion of your bank balance, and if so prints out one of a series of caustic comments on your credit-worthiness like:

THIS SPECIFICATION SEEMS TO BE
EXCEEDING YOUR CREDIT LIMIT

He also looks at how much profit he is likely to make on the sale so far, and if this drops too low he will start to lose interest and come up with comments like:

I HAVE AN URGENT APPOINTMENT

or

WE CLOSE IN FIVE MINUTES

At the same time he will be more helpful with regard to which of the available computers will fit your requirements, using PICK_COMPUTER which draws up a short list by comparing the rating given originally to this feature in the description of each computer with the value you put on it. The format for the descriptions (**Table 12.3**) is:

Table 12.3:   Computer Feature Ratings.

NAME	FEATURES																			
	1	2	3	4	5	6	7	8	9	10	11	12	13	14	15	16	17	18	19	20
JCN PC	7	8	8	9	8	8	8	0	9	9	7	7	0	7	6	8	8	9	9	9
KNACT SERIOUS	6	7	6	8	8	8	8	0	8	8	0	0	0	7	6	8	8	9	9	7
CLEARSIN MT	9	9	9	7	7	8	8	9	9	6	7	7	0	7	6	7	9	9	9	1
ACHRON ILLUSION	8	7	6	6	0	3	7	0	5	5	0	0	6	0	0	4	1	0	0	2
BANANA IIE	3	5	2	5	0	4	6	0	3	0	3	5	0	0	6	7	0	0	0	4
SI ELITE	8	8	8	7	7	8	8	0	7	2	7	4	0	0	6	0	0	0	0	0
COLECTOVISION CABBAGE	5	5	5	5	2	5	5	5	5	1	7	7	0	0	6	5	0	9	0	0
CANDY COLOURED COMPUTER	7	6	4	2	0	2	7	0	4	9	8	7	0	0	6	3	0	0	0	6
COMANDEAR 64	2	8	9	7	7	6	5	0	6	9	6	7	0	0	2	2	0	0	0	6
ATRIA 600GT	1	8	8	5	0	2	5	0	7	7	7	7	0	0	6	6	0	0	0	5

(name, value of feature 1, value of feature 2, value of feature 3, etc)

The highest-rated machine will always be picked out first but, if possible, at least three machines (possibly with lower ratings) will be selected, and the final choice made from them. Either the highest or lowest cost computer (at random) will be selected for mention, for example:

IF YOU WANT A REAL ROLLS-ROYCE
THEN JUST LOOK AT THE . . .

and

IF YOU ARE IN THE BUDGET MARKET
THEN WHAT ABOUT THE . . .

If only one machine fits the bill the program will come up with:

YOUR ONLY OPTION IS THE . . .

Computer Salesman

```
10 SCREEN
20 TITLE
30 SET_UP
40    REPeat QUESTION
50       PICK_QUESTION
60          IF FIND_slash THEN
70             LOOK_at
80             LOOK_and
90          END IF
100         IF FIND_ask THEN
110            JOIN_1
120         ELSE
130            JOIN_2
140         END IF
150       PRINT #3,PH$ & "?"
160       INPUT #0, IN$
170       IN$=" " & IN$
180       LD%=1
190       OF%=-1
200       FS%=1
210       NP%=0
220       RU%=0
```

```
230      M%=0
240      OM%=0
250      S1%=0
260      S2%=0
270        IF FIND_comma THEN
280          AND_OR_BUT
290            IN$=IN$(CM%+1 TO)
300        END IF
310      YES_PRESENT
320      NO_PRESENT
330      NT_PRESENT
340      DOUBLE_NEGATIVE
350      LIKES
360      DISLIKES
370      OBJECTS
380      ADVERBS
390      NEGATIVE_ADVERBS
400      ADJECTIVES
410      NEGATIVE_ADJECTIVES
420      CLS #1
430      CHEAP_EXPENSIVE
440        IF M%<1 THEN PRINT "PARDON, PLEASE
           EXCUSE   ME BUT" : NEXT QUESTION
450        IF OM%>1 THEN PRINT "HANG ON - ONE
           THING AT A TIME" : NEXT QUESTION
460      RULE_UPDATE
470      COST_PROFIT
480      SPENDING
490      PICK_COMPUTER
500      Q%=Q%+1
510        IF Q%>19 THEN Q%=0
520    END REPeat QUESTION
1000 DEFine PROCedure PICK_QUESTION
1010   PH%=RND(4 TO QP%)
1020   PH$=QP$(PH%)
1030 END DEFine PICK_QUESTION

2000 DEFine FuNction FIND_slash
2010   IS%="/" INSTR PH$
2020   RETurn IS%
2030 END DEFine FIND_slash

3000 DEFine PROCedure LOOK_at
```

```
3010    IF Q$(Q%,1)="@" THEN
3020      PH$=PH$(1 TO IS%-1) & "ARE" & PH$
          (IS% TO)
3030    END IF
3040 END DEFine LOOK_at

4000 DEFine PROCedure LOOK_and
4010    IF Q$(Q%,1)="&" THEN
4020      PH$=PH$(1 TO IS%-1) & "IS" & PH$
          (IS% TO)
4030    END IF
4040 END DEFine LOOK_and

5000 DEFine FuNction FIND_ask
5010    IS%="*" INSTR PH$
5020    RETurn IS%
5030 END DEFine FIND_ask

6000 DEFine PROCedure JOIN_1
6010    PH$=PH$(1 TO IS%-2) & " " & Q$(Q%)(2
        TO  LEN(Q$(Q%))) & PH$(IS%+1 TO)
6020 END DEFine JOIN_1

7000 DEFine PROCedure JOIN_2
7010    PH$=PH$ & " " & Q$(Q%)(2 TO LEN(Q$(Q%)))
7020 END DEFine JOIN_2

8000 DEFine FuNction FIND_comma
8010    CM%="," INSTR IN$
8020    RETurn CM%
8030 END DEFine FIND_comma

9000 DEFine PROCedure AND_OR_BUT
9010    IF FIND_AND + FIND_BUT THEN
9020      IF IN$(1 TO 3)=" NO" THEN
9030        R(Q%)=((R(Q%)*3)-3)/3
9040        IC(Q%)=((IC(Q%)*3)-(CR(Q%)*3))/3
9050        IP(Q%)=((IP(Q%)*3)-(PR(Q%)*3))/3
9060      ELSE
9070        R(Q%)=R(Q%)+1
9080        IC(Q%)=((IC(Q%)*3)+(CR(Q%)*3))/3
9090        IP(Q%)=((IP(Q%)*3)+(PR(Q%)*3))/3
9100      END IF
9110    END IF
9120 END DEFine AND_OR_BUT
```

```
10000 DEFine FuNction FIND_AND
10010   S1%="AND" INSTR IN$
10020   RETurn S1%
10030 END DEFine FIND_AND

11000 DEFine FuNction FIND_BUT
11010   S2%="BUT" INSTR IN$
11020   RETurn S2%
11030 END DEFine FIND_BUT

12000 DEFine PROCedure YES_PRESENT
12010   ST%=1
12020   I1$=IN$
12030     REPeat YES
12040       I1$=I1$(ST% TO)
12050       SP%="YES" INSTR I1$
12060         IF SP%=0 THEN RETurn
12070       RU%=RU%+1
12080       LD%=1
12090       M%=1
12100       ST%=SP%+1
12110     END REPeat YES
12120 END DEFine YES_PRESENT

13000 DEFine PROCedure NO_PRESENT
13010   ST%=1
13020   I1$=IN$
13030     REPeat NO
13040       I1$=I1$(ST% TO )
13050       SP%="NO" INSTR I1$
13060         IF SP%=0 THEN RETurn
13070           LD%=-1
13080           M%=1
13090           ST%=SP%+1
13100           NP%=NP%+1
13110     END REPeat NO
13120 END DEFine NO_PRESENT

14000 DEFine PROCedure NT_PRESENT
14010   ST%=1
14020   I1$=IN$
14030     REPeat NT
14040       I1$=I1$(ST% TO )
14050       SP%="N'T" INSTR I1$
```

```
14060           IF SP%=0 THEN RETurn
14070             LD%=-1
14080             M%=1
14090             ST%=SP%+1
14100             NP%=NP%+1
14110       END REPeat NT
14120 END DEFine NT_PRESENT


15000 DEFine PROCedure DOUBLE_NEGATIVE
15010    IF NP%=0 THEN RETurn
15020      IF NP% MOD 2 THEN
15030        RU%=((RU%*3)-3)/3
15040        LD%=-1
15050      ELSE
15060        RU%=RU%+1
15070        LD%=1
15080      END IF
15090 END DEFine DOUBLE_NEGATIVE

16000 DEFine PROCedure LIKES
16010    FOR N=0 TO LI%
16020      SP%=LI$(N) INSTR IN$
16030        IF SP%>0 THEN
16040          IF IN$(SP%-1)=" " THEN LD%=LD%*1
               : M%-1
16050        END IF
16060    END FOR N
16070 END DEFine LIKES

17000 DEFine PROCedure DISLIKES
17010    FOR N=0 TO DL%
17020      SP%=DL$(N) INSTR IN$
17030        IF SP%>0 THEN
17040          IF IN$(SP%-1)=" " THEN LD%=LD%*-1
               : RU%=RU*-1 : M%=1
17050        END IF
17060    END FOR N
17070 END DEFine DISLIKES

18000 DEFine PROCedure OBJECTS
18010    FOR N=0 TO OB%
18020      SP%=OB$(N) INSTR IN$
18030        IF SP%>0 THEN
```

```
18040            IF IN$(SP%-1)=" " THEN
                 RU%=((RU%*3)+(LD%*3))/3 : OF%=N :
                 M%=1 : OM%=OM%+1
18050        END IF
18060    END FOR N
18070 END DEFine OBJECTS

19000 DEFine PROCedure ADVERBS
19010    FOR N=0 TO AV%
19020      SP%=AV$(N) INSTR IN$
19030        IF SP%>0  THEN
19040            IF IN$(SP%-1)=" " THEN
                 RU%=((RU%*3)+(LD%*3))/3 : M%=1
19050        END IF
19060    END FOR N
19070 END DEFine ADVERBS

20000 DEFine PROCedure NEGATIVE_ADVERBS
20010    FOR N=0 TO NV%
20020      SP%=NV$(N) INSTR IN$
20030        IF SP%>0 THEN
20040            IF IN$(SP%-1)=" " THEN LD%=LD%*-1
                 : RU%=((RU%*3)+(LD%*3))/3 : M%=1
20050        END IF
20060    END FOR N
20070 END DEFine NEGATIVE_ADVERBS

21000 DEFine PROCedure ADJECTIVES
21010    FOR N=0 TO AJ%
21020      SP%=AJ$(N) INSTR IN$
21030        IF SP%>0 THEN
21040            IF IN$(SP%-1)=" " THEN
                 RU%=((RU%*3)+(LD%*3))/3 : M%=1
21050        END IF
21060    END FOR N
21070 END DEFine ADJECTIVES

22000 DEFine PROCedure NEGATIVE_ADJECTIVES
22010    FOR N=0 TO NJ%
22020      SP%=NJ$(N) INSTR IN$
22030        IF SP%>0 THEN
22040            IF IN$(SP%-1)=" " THEN LD%=LD%*-1
                 : RU%=((RU%*3)+(LD%*3))/3 : M%=1
```

```
22050        END IF
22060    END FOR N
22070 END DEFine NEGATIVE_ADJECTIVES

23000 DEFine PROCedure CHEAP_EXPENSIVE
23010   FOR N=0 TO HM%
23020     SP%=HM$(N) INSTR IN$
23030       IF SP%>0 THEN
23040         IF IN$(SP%-1)=" " THEN
23050           XX%=N
23060             IF XX%<2 THEN PRINT "CHEAP AND
                  NASTY"
23070             IF XX%>=2 THEN PRINT "RATHER
                  EXPENSIVE"
23080         END IF
23090       END IF
23100   END FOR N
23110 END DEFine CHEAP_EXPENSIVE

24000 DEFine PROCedure RULE_UPDATE
24010    IF OF%>-1 THEN
24020      R(OF%)=((R(OF%)*3)+(RU%*3))/3
24030      IC(OF%)=((IC(OF%)*3)+((CR(OF%)*RU%)
           *3))/3
24040      IP(OF%)=((IP(OF%)*3)+((PR(OF%)*RU%)
           *3))/3
24050    ELSE
24060      R(Q%)=((R(Q%)*3)+(RU%*3))/3
24070      IC(Q%)=((IC(Q%)*3)+((CR(Q%)*RU%)
           *3))/3
24080      IP(Q%)=((IP(Q%)*3)+((PR(Q%)*RU%)
           *3))/3
24090    END IF
24100    CLS #2
24110    PRINT #2,"DESIRE"
24120      FOR N=0 TO R%
24130        AT #2,N*3+15,0 : PRINT#2, R(N)
24140      END FOR N
24150    PRINT#2,"COST"
24160      FOR N=0 TO R%
24170        AT #2,N*3+15,1 : PRINT#2, IC(N)
24180      END FOR N
24190    PRINT#2,"PROFIT"
24200      FOR N=0 TO R%
```

```
24210        AT #2,N*3+15,2 : PRINT#2, IP(N)
24220     END FOR N
24230 END DEFine RULE_UPDATE

25000 DEFine PROCedure COST_PROFIT
25010    FOR N=0 TO OB%
25020       TC%=((TC%*3)+(IC(N)*3))/3
25030       TP%=((TP%*3)+(IP(N)*3))/3
25040    END FOR N
25050   PAPER #2,0 : INK #2,7 : CSIZE #2,1,0
25060   PRINT #2,"    TOTAL COST ";TC%;"    TOTAL
        PROFIT ";TP%;"  BANK BALANCE ";BB%;
25070   PAPER #2,4 : INK #2,0 : CSIZE #2,0,0
25080 END DEFine COST_PROFIT

26000 DEFine PROCedure SPENDING
26010    IF TP%<Q%*5 THEN TX%=RND(EX%) : INK
         #1,4 : PRINT \EX$(TX%) : INK #1,0
26020    IF TC%>BB%/(Q%+1) THEN PT%=RND(CS%) :
         INK #1,2 : PRINT \CS$(PT%) : INK #1,0
26030    TC%=0
26040    TP%=0
26050 END DEFine SPENDING-

27000 DEFine PROCedure PICK_COMPUTER
27010   FOR X=9 TO 0 STEP -1
27020      PO$=""
27030        FOR N=0 TO CO%
27040           IF ((FE(N,Q%)*3)-(R(Q%)*3))>X THEN
                 PO$=PO$ & N : M%=N
27050        END FOR N
27060         IF LEN(PO$)<3 THEN END FOR X
27070      TS%=0
27080      BS%=10
27090        FOR CH=0 TO LEN(PO$)-1
27100           NC%=PO$(CH+1)
27110              IF C(NC%)>=TS% THEN TS%=C(NC%)
                   : HI%=NC%
27120              IF C(NC%)<=BS% THEN BS%=C(NC%)
                   : LO%=NC%
27130         END FOR CH
27140           IF HI%=LO% THEN
27150              PRINT #1,"YOUR ONLY OPTION IS
                   THE"
```

```
27160              CSIZE #1,2,1 : PRINT #1," ***
                   ** ";CO$(HI%);" ***** "; :
                   CSIZE #1,2,0
27170              RETurn
27180            END IF
27190          FI$=CO$(HI%)
27200          LA$=CO$(LO%)
27210          SE%=RND(1 TO 2)
27220          SL%=RND(2)
27230            IF SE%<>2 THEN
27240              PRINT #1,HI$(SL%) : CSIZE
                   #1,2,1 : PRINT #1," ***** "
                   ;FI$;" *****";: CSIZE #1,2,0
27250            ELSE
27260              PRINT #1,LO$(SL%) : CSIZE
                   #1,2,1 : PRINT #1," ***** "
                   ;LA$;" *****";: CSIZE #1,2,0
27270            END IF
27280 END DEFine PICK_COMPUTER

28000 DEFine PROCedure SCREEN
28010    MODE 4
28020    WINDOW #0,470,40,25,215
28030    BORDER #0,5,4
28040    PAPER #0,0
28050    INK #0,7
28060    CSIZE #0,2,0
28070    CLS #0
28080    WINDOW #1,470,105,25,90
28090    BORDER #1,5,4
28100    PAPER #1,7
28110    INK #1,0
28120    CSIZE #1,2,0
28130    CLS #1
28140    WINDOW #2,470,50,25,15
28150    BORDER #2,5,4
28160    PAPER #2,4
28170    INK #2,0
28180    CSIZE #2,0,0
28190    CLS #2
28200    OPEN #3,SCR_470X20A25X195
28210    BORDER #3,5,4
28220    PAPER #3,7
28230    INK #3,0
```

```
28240    CSIZE #3,2,0
28250    CLS #3
28260    OPEN #4,SCR_470X25A25X65
28270    BORDER #4,2,2
28280    PAPER #4,2
28290    INK #4,7
28300    CSIZE #4,2,1
28310    CLS #4
28320 END DEFine SCREEN


29000 DEFine PROCedure TITLE
29010    PRINT #4," $$$$$    MULTIMEGA MICROSTORE
            $$$$$";
29020 END DEFine TITLE


30000 DEFine PROCedure SET_UP
30010    RESTORE
30020    QP%=5
30030    Q%=19
30040    R%=Q%
30050    OB%=Q%
30060    AJ%=7
30070    AV%=4
30080    LI%=3
30090    DL%=3
30100    NJ%=8
30110    NV%=2
30120    HM%=3
30130    BB%=100
30140    CO%=9
30150    FE%=19
30160    CT%=9
30170    HI%=2
30180    LO%=2
30190    CS%=2
30200    EX%=2
30210    TC%=0
30220    TP%=0
30230    DIM OB$(OB%,10)
30240    DIM AJ$(AJ%,6)
30250    DIM NJ$(NJ%,7)
30260    DIM AV$(AV%,6)
30270    DIM NV$(NV%,6)
```

```
30280    DIM LI$(LI%,7)
30290    DIM DL$(DL%,7)
30300    DIM Q$(Q%,20)
30310    DIM QP$(QP%,16)
30320    DIM HM$(HM%,20)
30330    DIM R(R%)
30340    DIM CR(Q%)
30350    DIM PR(Q%)
30360    DIM IC(Q%)
30370    DIM IP(Q%)
30380    DIM CO$(CO%,30)
30390    DIM FE(CO%,FE%)
30400    DIM DF(CO%,FE%)
30410    DIM C(CT%)
30420    DIM CS$(CS%,100)
30430    DIM EX$(EX%,100)
30440    DIM HI$(HI%,100)
30450    DIM LO$(LO%,100)
30460    DATA "BASIC","GRAPHIC","SOUND",
         "KEYBOARD","FUNCTION","MEMORY",
         "TAPE","MACRODRIVE","DISC"
30470    DATA "SOFTWARE","CARTRIDGE",
         "JOYSTICK","ASSEMBL","CENTRONIC",
         "RS232","EXPAND"
30480    DATA "NETWORK","16-BIT","MULTITASK",
         "SERVICE"
30490    DATA "GOOD","EXCEL","SUPER","MAGNIF",
         "FIRST","FAST","ESSENT","LOT"
30500    DATA "BAD","RUBBISH","POOR","SLOW",
         "INEFFIC","FEW","WORS","LEAST","LESS"
30510    DATA "REAL","VERY","OFTEN","NECESS",
         "TRU"
30520    DATA "NEVER","UNNECES","INFREQ"
30530    DATA "WANT","LIKE","NEED","REQUIRE"
30540    DATA "HATE","DISLIKE","LOATHE","DETEST"
30550    DATA "&GOOD BASIC",5,2,"@GRAPHICS",7,2,
         "&SOUND",6,2,"&A GOOD KEYBOARD",4,2
30560    DATA "@FUNCTION KEYS",1,5,"&A LARGE
         MEMORY",3,6,"&A TAPE INTERFACE",2,2
30570    DATA "@MACRODRIVES",2,4,"@DISCS",5,8,
         "&EXTENSIVE SOFTWARE",0,9
30580    DATA "&A CARTRIDGE PORT",1,6,"&A
         JOYSTICK PORT",1,7,"&AN ASSEMBLER",2,1
```

```
30590    DATA "&A CENTRONICS PORT",2,5,"&AN RS232
         PORT",2,6,"&EXPANDABILITY",2,9,
         "&NETWORKING",3,4
30600    DATA "&A 16-BIT CPU",1,7,"&MULTITASKING"
         ,5,5,"&GOOD SERVICE",1,9
30610    DATA "WOULD YOU LIKE","WHAT ABOUT","HOW
         ABOUT","DO YOU WANT","DO YOU REQUIRE",
         "/* IMPORTANT"
30620    DATA "CHEAP","INEXPENSIVE"
30630    DATA "DEAR","EXPENSIVE"
30640    DATA "JCN PC",7,8,8,9,8,8,8,0,9,9,7,7,0
         ,7,6,8,8,9,9,9
30650    DATA "KNACT SERIOUS",6,7,6,8,8,8,8,0,8,
         8,0,0,0,7,6,8,8,9,9,7
30660    DATA "CLEARSIN MT",9,9,9,7,7,8,8,9,9,6,7
         ,7,0,7,6,7,9,9,9,1
30670    DATA "ACHRON ILLUSION",8,7,6,6,0,3,7,0,
         5,5,0,0,6,0,0,4,1,0,0,2
30680    DATA "BANANA IIE",3,5,2,5,0,4,6,0,3,0,3
         ,5,0,0,6,7,0,0,0,4
30690    DATA "SI ELITE",8,8,8,7,7,8,8,0,7,2,7,
         4,0,0,6,0,0,0,0,0
30700    DATA "COLECTOVISION CABBAGE",5,5,5,5,
         2,5,5,5,5,1,7,7,0,0,6,5,0,9,0,0
30710    DATA "CANDY COLOURED COMPUTER",7,6,4,2,
         0,2,7,0,4,9,8,7,0,0,6,3,0,0,0,6
30720    DATA "COMANDEAR 64",2,8,9,7,7,6,5,0,6
         ,9,6,7,0,0,2,2,0,0,0,6
30730    DATA "ATRIA 600GT",1,8,8,5,0,2,5,0,7,7,
         7,7,0,0,6,6,0,0,0,5
30740    DATA 10,9,8,7,6,5,4,3,2,1
30750    DATA "I THINK YOU ARE GETTING OUT OF
         YOUR  PRICE RANGE"
30760    DATA "THIS SPECIFICATION SEEMS TO BE
         EXCEEDING YOUR CREDIT LIMIT"
30770    DATA "I DON'T THINK THAT YOU CAN AFFORD
         SUCH LUXURIES"
30780    DATA "EXCUSE ME, I CAN HEAR THE PHONE
         RINGING"
30790    DATA "I HAVE AN URGENT APPOINTMENT"
30800    DATA "WE CLOSE IN FIVE MINUTES"
30810    DATA "IF YOU ARE IN THE BUDGET MARKET
         THEN WHAT ABOUT THE ","AN INEXPENSIVE
         CHOICE IS THE"
```

```
30820    DATA "YOU GET GOOD VALUE FOR MONEY WITH
         THE"
30830    DATA "IF YOU WANT A FIRST CLASS PRODUCT
         THEN YOU MUST TRY THE"
30840    DATA "FOR STATE OF THE ART TECHNOLOGY
         YOU  CAN'T BEAT THE"
30850    DATA "IF YOU WANT A ROLLS ROYCE THEN
         JUST  LOOK AT THE"
30860      FOR N=0 TO OB%
30870        READ OB$(N)
30880      END FOR N
30890      FOR N=0 TO AJ%
30900        READ AJ$(N)
30910      END FOR N
30920      FOR N=0 TO NJ%
30930        READ NJ$(N)
30940      END FOR N
30950      FOR N=0 TO AV%
30960        READ AV$(N)
30970      END FOR N
30980      FOR N=0 TO NV%
30990        READ NV$(N)
31000      END FOR N
31010      FOR N=0 TO LI%
31020        READ LI$(N)
31030      END FOR N
31040      FOR N=0 TO DL%
31050        READ DL$(N)
31060      END FOR N
31070      FOR N=0 TO Q%
31080        READ Q$(N)
31090        READ CR(N)
31100        READ PR(N)
31110      END FOR N
31120      FOR N=0 TO QP%
31130        READ QP$(N)
31140      END FOR N
31150      FOR N=0 TO HM%
31160        READ HM$(N)
31170      END FOR N
31180      FOR N=0 TO CO%
31190        READ CO$(N)
31200        FOR M=0 TO FE%
31210          READ FE(N,M)
```

```
31220         END FOR M
31230      END FOR N
31240      FOR N=0 TO CT%
31250         READ C(N)
31260      END FOR N
31270      FOR N=0 TO CS%
31280         READ CS$(N)
31290      END FOR N
31300      FOR N=0 TO EX%
31310         READ EX$(N)
31320      END FOR N
31330      FOR N=0 TO LO%
31340         READ LO$(N)
31350      END FOR N
31360      FOR N=0 TO HI%
31370         READ HI$(N)
31380      END FOR N
31390      Q%=0
31400 END DEFine SET_UP

32000 DEFine PROCedure XX
32010    WINDOW #2,470,240,25,15
32020    PAPER #2,7
32030    INK #2,0
32040    CLS #2
32050 END  DEFine XX
```

The rest is up to you

Artificial intelligence is a fascinating subject and we trust that we have given you enough information to get you started on your own experiments in this area. We have certainly enjoyed making our own explorations whilst putting this book together but we have started to wonder how long it will be before someone designs an expert system program which writes books. . . .

Other titles from Sunshine

SPECTRUM BOOKS

Artificial Intelligence on the Spectrum Computer
Keith & Steven Brain   ISBN 0 946408 37 8   **£6.95**

Spectrum Adventures
Tony Bridge & Roy Carnell   ISBN 0 946408 07 6   **£5.95**

Machine Code Sprites and Graphics for the ZX Spectrum
John Durst   ISBN 0 946408 51 3   **£6.95**

ZX Spectrum Astronomy
Maurice Gavin   ISBN 0 946408 24 6   **£6.95**

Spectrum Machine Code Applications
David Laine   ISBN 0 946408 17 3   **£6.95**

The Working Spectrum
David Lawrence   ISBN 0 946408 00 9   **£5.95**

Inside Your Spectrum
Jeff Naylor & Diane Rogers   ISBN 0 946408 35 1   **£6.95**

Master your ZX Microdrive
Andrew Pennell   ISBN 0 946408 19 X   **£6.95**

COMMODORE 64 BOOKS

Graphic Art for the Commodore 64
Boris Allan   ISBN 0 946408 15 7   **£5.95**

DIY Robotics and Sensors on the Commodore Computer
John Billingsley   ISBN 0 946408 30 0   **£6.95**

Artificial Intelligence on the Commodore 64
Keith & Steven Brain   ISBN 0 946408 29 7   **£6.95**

Simulation Techniques on the Commodore 64
John Cochrane   ISBN 0 946408 58 0   **£6.95**

Machine Code Graphics and Sound for the Commodore 64
Mark England & David Lawrence   ISBN 0 946408 28 9   **£6.95**

Commodore 64 Adventures
Mike Grace   ISBN 0 946408 11 4   **£5.95**

Business Applications for the Commodore 64
James Hall   ISBN 0 946408 12 2   **£5.95**

Mathematics on the Commodore 64
Czes Kosniowski   ISBN 0 946408 14 9   **£5.95**

Advanced Programming Techniques on the Commodore 64
David Lawrence   ISBN 0 946408 23 8   **£5.95**

Commodore 64 Disk Companion
David Lawrence & Mark England   ISBN 0 946408 49 1   **£7.95**
The Working Commodore 64
David Lawrence   ISBN 0 946408 02 5   **£5.95**
Commodore 64 Machine Code Master
David Lawrence & Mark England   ISBN 0 946408 05 X   **£6.95**
Machine Code Games Routines for the Commodore 64
Paul Roper   ISBN 0 946408 47 5   **£6.95**
Programming for Education on the Commodore 64
John Scriven & Patrick Hall   ISBN 0 946408 27 0   **£5.95**
Writing Strategy Games on your Commodore 64
John White   ISBN 0 946408 54 8   **£6.95**

ELECTRON BOOKS

Graphic Art for the Electron Computer
Boris Allan   ISBN 0 946408 20 3   **£5.95**
Programming for Education on the Electron Computer
John Scriven & Patrick Hall   ISBN 0 946408 21 1   **£5.95**

BBC COMPUTER BOOKS

Functional Forth for the BBC Computer
Boris Allan   ISBN 0 946408 04 1   **£5.95**
Graphic Art for the BBC Computer
Boris Allan   ISBN 0 946408 08 4   **£5.95**
DIY Robotics and Sensors for the BBC Computer
John Billingsley   ISBN 0 946408 13 0   **£6.95**
Essential Maths on the BBC and Electron Computer
Czes Kosniowski   ISBN 0 946408 34 3   **£5.95**
Programming for Education on the BBC Computer
John Scriven & Patrick Hall   ISBN 0 946408 10 6   **£5.95**
Making Music on the BBC Computer
Ian Waugh   ISBN 0 946408 26 2   **£5.95**

DRAGON BOOKS

Advanced Sound & Graphics for the Dragon
Keith & Steven Brain   ISBN 0 946408 06 8   **£5.95**
Artificial Intelligence on the Dragon Computer
Keith & Steven Brain   ISBN 0 946408 33 5   **£6.95**
Dragon 32 Games Master
Keith & Steven Brain   ISBN 0 946408 03 3   **£5.95**
The Working Dragon
David Lawrence   ISBN 0 946408 01 7   **£5.95**
The Dragon Trainer
Brian Lloyd   ISBN 0 946408 09 2   **£5.95**

ATARI BOOKS

Atari Adventures
Tony Bridge   ISBN 0 946408 18 1   **£5.95**
Writing Strategy Games on your Atari Computer
John White   ISBN 0 946408 22 X   **£5.95**

SINCLAIR QL BOOKS

Introduction to Simulation Techniques on the Sinclair QL
John Cochrane   ISBN 0 946408 45 9   **£6.95**
Quill, Easel, Archive & Abacus on the Sinclair QL
Alison McCallum-Varcy   ISBN 0 946408 55 6   **£6.95**

GENERAL BOOKS

Home Applications on your Micro
Mike Grace   ISBN 0 946408 50 5   **£6.95**

Sunshine also publishes

POPULAR COMPUTING WEEKLY

The first weekly magazine for home computer users. Each copy contains Top 10 charts of the best-selling software and books and up-to-the-minute details of the latest games. Other features in the magazine include regular hardware and software reviews, programming hints, computer swap, adventure corner and pages of listings for the Spectrum, Dragon, BBC, VIC 20 and 64, ZX 81 and other popular micros. Only 40p a week, a year's subscription costs £19.95 (£9.98 for six months) in the UK and £37.40 (£18.70 for six months) overseas.

DRAGON USER

The monthly magazine for all users of Dragon microcomputers. Each issue contains reviews of software and peripherals, programming advice for beginners and advanced users, program listings, a technical advisory service and all the latest news related to the Dragon. A year's subscription (12 issues) costs £10 in the UK and £16 overseas.

MICRO ADVENTURER

The monthly magazine for everyone interested in Adventure games, war gaming and simulation/role-playing games. Includes reviews of all the latest software, lists of all the software available and programming advice. A year's subscription (12 issues) costs £10 in the UK and £16 overseas.

COMMODORE HORIZONS

The monthly magazine for all users of Commodore computers. Each issue contains reviews of software and peripherals, programming advice for beginners and advanced users, program listings, a technical advisory service and all the latest news. A year's subscription costs £10 in the UK and £16 overseas.

For further information contact:
Sunshine
12–13 Little Newport Street
London WC2R 3LD
01-437 4343

Telex: 296275